Super Cheap New York Travel Guide

"The skyline of New York is a monument of a splendor that no pyramids or palaces will ever equal or approach." - Ayn Rand.

Our Mission

Did you know you can fly on a private jet for $500? Yes, a fully private jet. Complete with flutes of champagne and reclinable creamy leather seats. Your average billionaire spends $20,00 on the exact same flight. You can get it for $500 when you book private jet empty leg flights. Amazed? Don't be. This is just one of thousands of ways you can travel luxuriously on a budget.

When our brain hears the word "budget" it hears deprivation, suffering, agony, even depression. But budget travel need not be synonymous with hostels and pack lunches. You can enjoy an incredible and luxurious trip to New York on a budget, just like you can enjoy a private jet flight for 10% of the normal cost when you know how. The past years have shown us travel is a gift we must cherish. We believe strongly that this gift is best enjoyed on a budget. Together with thrifty locals, we have funneled our passion for travel bargains into Super Cheap New York.

Our passion is finding travel bargains. This doesn't mean doing less or sleeping in hostels. Someone who spends A LOT on travel hasn't planned or wants to spend their money. We promise you that with a bit of planning, you can experience a luxury trip to New York on a budget.

Traveling need not be expensive; Travel guides, Travel agents, Travel bloggers and influencers often show you overpriced accommodation, restaurants and big-ticket attractions because they earn commission from your "we're on vacation" mentality, which often leads to reckless spending. Our mission is to teach you how to enjoy more for less and get the best value from every dollar you spend in New York.

Taking a trip to New York is not just an outer journey, it's an inner one. Budget travel brings you closer to locals, culture and authenticity; which makes your inner journey more fulfilling. Super Cheap New York will save you 1000 times what you paid for it while teaching you local tips and tricks. We have formulated a system to pass on to you, so you can enjoy a luxurious trip to New York without the nightmare credit card bill.

Our mission is to dispel myths, save you tons of money, give you the local tips and tricks and help you find experiences in New York that will flash before your eyes when you come to take your last breath on this beautiful earth.

Who this book is for and why anyone can enjoy budget travel

There is a big difference between being cheap and frugal. Who doesn't like to spend money on beautiful experiences?

Over 20 years of travel has taught me I could have a 20 cent experience that will stir my soul more than a $100 one. Of course, sometimes the reverse is true, my point is, spending money on travel is the best investment you can make but it doesn't have to be at levels set by hotels and attractions with massive ad spends and influencers who are paid small fortunes to get you to buy into something you could have for a fraction of the cost.

This book is for those who want to have the cold hard budget busting facts to hand (which is why we've included so many one page charts, which you can use as a quick reference), but otherwise, the book provides plenty of tips to help you shape your own New York experience.

We have designed these travel guides to give you a unique planning tool to experience an unforgettable trip without spending the ascribed tourist budget.

This guide focuses on New York's unbelievable bargains. Of course, there is little value in traveling to New York and not experiencing everything it has to offer. Where possible, we've included cheap workarounds or listed the experience in the Loved but Costly section.

When it comes to FUN budget travel, it's all about what you know. You can have all the feels without most of the bills. A few days spent planning can save you thousands. Luckily, we've done the planning for you, so you can distill the information in minutes not days, leaving you to focus on what matters: immersing yourself in the sights, sounds and smells of New York, meeting awesome new people and feeling relaxed and happy. I sincerely hope our tips will bring you great joy at a fraction of the price you expected.

So, grab a cup of tea or coffee, put your feet up and relax; you're about to enter the world of enjoying New York on the cheap. Oh, and don't forget a biscuit. You need energy to plan a trip of a lifetime on a budget.

Super Cheap New York is <u>not</u> for travellers with the following needs:

1. You require a book with detailed offline travel maps. Super Cheap Insider Guides are best used with Google Maps - download before you travel to make the most of your time and money.
2. You would like thousands of accommodation, food and attraction recommendations; by definition, cheapest is often singular. We only include maximum value recommendations. We purposively leave out over-priced attractions when there is no workaround.
3. You would like detailed write-ups about hotels/Airbnbs/ Restaurants. We are bargain hunters first and foremost. We dedicate our time to finding the best deals, not writing flowery language about their interiors. Plus, things change. If I had a pound for every time I'd read a Lonely Planet description only to find the place totally different, I would be a rich man. Always look at online reviews for the latest up-to-date information.

If you want to save A LOT of money while comfortably enjoying an unforgettable trip to New York, minus the marketing, hype, scams and tourist traps read on.

Redefining Super Cheap

The value you get out of Super Cheap New York is not based on what you paid for it; it's based on what you do with it. You can only do great things with it if you believe saving money is worth your time. Charging things to your credit card and thinking 'oh I'll pay it off when I get home' is something you won't be tempted to do if you change your beliefs now. Think about what you associate with the word cheap, because you make your beliefs and your beliefs make you.

I grew up thinking you had to spend more than you could afford to have a good time traveling. Now I've visited 190 countries, I know nothing is further from the truth. Before you embark upon reading our specific tips for New York think about your associations with the word cheap.

Here are the dictionary definitions of cheap:

- Costing very little; relatively low in price; inexpensive: a cheap dress.
- costing little labor or trouble: Words are cheap.
- charging low prices: a very cheap store.
- Of little account; of small value; mean; shoddy: Cheap conduct; cheap workmanship.
- Embarrassed; sheepish: He felt cheap about his mistake.
- Stingy; miserly: He's too cheap to buy his own brother a cup of coffee.

Three out of six definitions have extremely negative connotations. The 'super cheap' we're talking about in this book is not shoddy, embarrassed, or stingy.
We added the super to reinforce our message. Super's dictionary definition stands for 'a super quality'. Super Cheap stands for enjoying the best on the lowest budget. Question other people's definitions of cheap so you're not blinded to possibilities, poten-

tial, and prosperity. Here are some new associations to consider forging:

Shoddy

Cheap stuff doesn't last is an adage marketing companies have drilled into consumers. However, by asking vendors the right questions cheap doesn't mean something won't last. I had a $10 backpack last for 8 years and a $100 suitcase bust on the first journey.

A study out of San Francisco University found that people who spent money on experiences rather than things were happier. Memories last forever, not things, even expensive things. And as we will show you during this guide, you don't need to pay to create glorious memories.[1]

Embarrassed

I have friends who routinely pay more to vendors because they think their money is putting food on this person's table. Paradoxically, Cuban doctors are driving taxis because they earn more money; it's not always a good thing for the place you're visiting to pay more and can cause unwanted distortion in their culture - Airbnb pushing out renters is an obvious example. Think carefully about whether the extra money is helping people or incentivising greed.

Stingy

Cheap can be eco-friendly. Buying thrift clothes is cheap, but you also help the Earth. Many travellers are often disillusioned by the reality of traveling since the places on our bucket-lists are over-crowded. Cheap can take you away from the crowds. You can find balance and harmony being cheap. "Remember a journey is

---

[1]   Paulina Pchelin & Ryan T. Howell (2014) The hidden cost of value-seeking: People do not accurately forecast the economic benefits of experiential purchases, The Journal of Positive Psychology, 9:4, 322-334, DOI: 10.1080/17439760.2014.898316

best measured in friends, rather than miles." – Tim Cahill. And making friends is free!

A recent survey by Credit Karma found 50% of Millennials and Gen Z get into debt traveling. **Please don't allow credit card debt to be an unwanted souvenir you take home.** As you will see from this book, there's so much you can enjoy in New York for free, some many unique bargains and so many ways to save money! You just need to want to!

Discover New York

Magnetic, electric and Diverse. New York is Tall, Unforgettable, Intense, Intoxicating and utterly Addictive. But even
these adjectives do not do New York justice. It is the kind of
place thats difficult to describe and many people will rightly
conclude by saying "you just have to go".

New York was founded by the Dutch in 1624 they named it
'New Amsterdam'. In 1664 the British took control and re-
named it New York. Today New York is just like it is in the
movies: horns honked by yellow cab drivers, street corners
inhabited by hot dog vendors and fashionata's walk the
streets Sex and The City style.
The first time you walk around Times Square you will wonder if you are in a New York movie.
8.6 million people call the largest city in the USA home
among them 78 billionaires. New York is made up of five
boroughs: Manhattan, The Bronx, Queens, Brooklyn, and
Staten Island. Despite the Billionaires, New York offers a
wealth of opportunities to experience the city for free or
cheap, from strolls through the city streets marvelling at the
skyscrapers to free museums, exhibitions, public buildings,

parks and churches, as well as fabulous cheap eats in Chinatown, Little Italy and Soho. There's so much to see and do that you will be planning your second visit.

Like any city that caters to tourists New York can quickly empty your wallet but take heart, the trick to keeping your trip affordable is to get off the tourist track and find the local deals. Use this guide to make sure New York leaves a lasting impression on your heart and mind, not your bank balance. If you follow the advice in this guide you could definitely get away with spending about $60 a day including accommodation.

Some of New York's Best Bargains

Kayak for free

Hire a free kayak from the Boathouse at Brooklyn Bridge Park on Wednesdays, Thursdays and Saturdays through summer. https://www.brooklynbridgepark.org/

Watch a Baseball game on the cheap

Baseball is any self-respecting New Yorkers passion. 162 Baseball games are played between April and October. Whether you choose to support The New York Yankees or The New York Mets you can score tickets for a paltry $15! You can book cheap tickets here: https://gametime.co/new-york-yankees-tickets

If basketball is more your thing head to The West 4th Street Basketball Courts in Greenwich Village, known informally as "The Cage". This is where scouts go to find the next Micheal Jordan.

Enjoy Free events and activities

On about any day of the year, you can find something fun, informative, healthy and FREE to enjoy in a New York park. NYC Parks is the ultimate source of free outdoor events. See whats on during your visit https://www.nycgovparks.org/events

Time Out NYC also maintain a list of free events happening around the city: https://www.timeout.com/newyork/things-to-do/free-things-to-do-today

Do a free tour of Grand Central

The Municipal Arts Society of New York conduct daily free 75minute tours of Grand Central Station at 12.30pm (the meeting point is the information booth on the Grand Concourse). For more information visit www.mas.org

Dine on delicious Korean

Danji serves the best bulgogi beef sliders in New York. You can get a lunch menu for a mere $13, dinner menu from $23 and a tasting menu, with all of the best options on the menu for $55. Address: 346 W 52nd Street

Take advantage of Fleet Week

During the last-week of May; when sailors invade New York you can take free tours of ships arriving from all across the globe.

Do a free tour of Liberty Island

Park Rangers lead free tours on the island home to the Statue of Liberty. Tours are 40 minutes. The tours chronicle the islands history during 1892 and 1924; the busiest years of immigration.

Do a free tour of New York Distilling Company

Brooklyn Brewery offers free tours, weekends between noon and 6pm. For an up-to-date schedule visit www.brooklyn-brewery.com.

Like your libations? Here are the Best Happy Hours in New York:

- 169 Bar.
- Bonnie Vee.
- Fresh Salt.
- Huertas.
- Mister Paradise.
- The Mermaid Inn.
- Alfie's Kitchen & Craft Beer Bar.
- Fools Gold NYC.

Visit during restaurant week

If you're a foodie, visit during NYC Restaurant Week. A biannual event that has been held every summer and winter since 1992. Back then, only a few restaurants took part in the promotion, while this year's event has over 500 participating restaurants . Over time, the length of Restaurant Week has been extended so that we can now enjoy almost a full month of great, affordable food instead of just a week. Many of New York's top chefs - Jean-Georges Vongerichten, Daniel Boulud, Marcus Samuelsson and Leah Cohen cook during the week. There are 3 price options at NYC Restaurant Weeks 2023: $30 (for lunch), $45 (for dinner) and $60 (for both). they're spread across all five boroughs (with the majority being in Manhattan). The the Winter one takes place from mid-January to mid-February, and the Summer one from mid-July to mid-August. Reserve your tables in advance: https://www.nycgo.com/restaurant-week

How to Enjoy ALLOCATING Money in New York

'Money's greatest intrinsic value—and this can't be overstated—is its ability to give you control over your time.' - Morgan Housel

Notice I have titled the chapter how to enjoy allocating money in New York. I'll use saving and allocating interchangeably in the book, but since most people associate saving to feel like a turtleneck, that's too tight, I've chosen to use wealth language. Rich people don't save. They allocate. What's the difference? Saving can feel like something you don't want or wish to do and allocating has your personal will attached to it.

And on that note, it would be helpful if you considered removing the following words and phrase from your vocabulary for planning and enjoying your New York trip:

- Wish

- Want

- Maybe someday

These words are part of poverty language. Language is a dominant source of creation. Use it to your advantage. You don't have to wish, want or say maybe someday to New York. You can enjoy the same things millionaires enjoy in New York without the huge spend.

'People don't like to be sold-but they love to buy.' - Jeffrey Gitomer.

Every good salesperson who understands the quote above places obstacles in the way of their clients' buying. Companies create waiting lists, restaurants pay people to queue outside in order to create demand. People reason if something is so in demand, it must be worth having but that's often just marketing. Take this sales maxim 'People don't like to be sold-but they love to buy and flip it on its head to allocate your money in New York on things YOU desire. You love to spend and hate to be sold. That means when something comes your way, it's not 'I can't afford it,' it's 'I don't want it' or maybe 'I don't want it right now'.

Saving money doesn't mean never buying a latte, never taking a taxi, never taking vacations (of course, you bought this book). Only you get to decide on how you spend and on what. Not an advice columnist who thinks you can buy a house if you never eat avocado toast again.

I love what Kate Northrup says about affording something: "If you really wanted it you would figure out a way to get it. If it were that VALUABLE to you, you would make it happen."

I believe if you master the art of allocating money to bargains, it can feel even better than spending it! Bold claim, I know. But here's the truth: Money gives you freedom and options. The more you keep in your account and or invested the more freedom and options you'll have. The principal reason you should save and allocate money is TO BE FREE! Remember, a trip's main purpose is relaxation, rest and enjoyment, aka to feel free.

When you talk to most people about saving money on vacation. They grimace. How awful they proclaim not to go wild on your vacation. If you can't get into a ton of debt enjoying your once-in-a-lifetime vacation, when can you?

When you spend money 'theres's a sudden rush of dopamine which vanishes once the transaction is complete. What happens in the brain when you save money? It increases feelings of security and peace. You don't need to stress life's uncertainties. And having a greater sense of peace can actually help you save more money.' Stressed out people make impulsive financial choices, calm people don't.'

The secret to enjoying saving money on vacation is very simple: never save money from a position of lack. Don't think 'I wish I could afford that'. Choose not to be marketed to. Choose not to consume at a price others set. Don't save money from the flawed premise you don't have enough. Don't waste your time living in the box that society has created, which says saving money on vacation means sacrifice. It doesn't.

Traveling to New York can be an expensive endeavor if you don't approach it with a plan, but you have this book which is packed with tips. The biggest other asset is your perspective.

How to feel RICH in New York

You don't need millions in your bank to **feel rich**. Feeling rich feels different to every person.

"Researchers have pooled data on the relationship between money and emotions from more than 1.6 million people across 162 countries and found that **wealthier people feel more positive "self-regard emotions" such as confidence, pride and determination.**"

Here are things to see, do and taste in New York, that will have you overflowing with gratitude for your luxury trip to New York.

- Achieving a Michelin Star rating is the most coveted accolade for restaurants but those that obtain a Michelin Star are synonymous with high cost, but in New York there are restaurants with Michelin-stars offering lunch menus for 30 dollars or less! If you want to taste the finest seasonal local dishes while dining in pure luxury, here are the 8 Most Affordable Michelin Restaurants in New York:

- Casa Enrique I $47 per person.
- Claro I $48 per person.
- Oxomoco I $50 per person.
- Contra I $53 per person.
- Meadowsweet I $55 per person.
- Don Angie I $55 per person.
- The Musket Room I $55 per person.
- Rezdôra I $60 per person.

If fine dining isn't your thing, don't worry further on in the guide you will find a range of delicious cheap eats in New York that deserve a Michelin-Star.

- While money can't buy happiness, it can buy cake and isn't that sort of the same thing? Jokes aside, Fay Da Bakery (83 Mott St) is a Chinese Bakery in New York have turned cakes and pastries into edible art.

- While you might not be staying in a penthouse, you can still enjoy the same views. Visit rooftop bars in New York, like Cantina Rooftop to enjoy incredible sunset views for the price of just one drink. And if you want to continue enjoying libations, head over to 169 Bar for a dirt-cheap happy hour, lots of reasonably priced (and delicious) cocktails and cheap delicious snacks.

- Walking out of a salon or barber shop with a fresh cut makes most people feel rich. As the maxim goes, if you look good, you feel good. If you crave that freshly blow-dried or trimmed look, become a hair model salonmodel.co in New York. You'll receive a completely free cut/colour or wash. Of course, always agree on the look with your stylist.

Those are just some ideas for you to know that visiting New York on a budget doesn't have to feel like sacrifice or constriction. Now let's get into the nuts and bolts of New York on the super cheap.

Planning your trip

When to visit

The first step in saving money on your New York trip is timing. If you are not tied to school holidays, the best time to visit is during the shoulder-season months April to June and September to early November when the weather is warmer but the tourist crowds are fewer. The cheapest time to visit New York is on weekends from mid-January to the end of February but winter weather can be extreme.
In the summer take advantage of rooftop movies, and concerts on the beach at Coney Island and free yoga in Bryant Park. Don't despair if you are visiting during peak times there are innumerable hacks to save on accommodation in New York which we will go into detail on.

When you visit will determine the luxury level of your accommodation. If staying in a five-star hotel is a must for you in NYC, then arrange your visit for the low season or shoulder months.

AVOID The weekend price hike in peak season

Hostel and hotel prices skyrocket during weekends in peak season. If you can get out of New York for the weekend if you visit in the peak season you'll save $$$ on your accommodation. For example a dorm room at a popular Hostel costs $44 a night during the week. That price goes to $253 for Saturday's and Sundays.

Visit New York on your birthday

Companies know rewarding customers on their birthdays will boost retention so many in New York go out of their way to surprise customers and make them feel special on their birthdays.

Visit New York on your birthday you can get well over $250 of free stuff, meals, cakes and more. All you need is a valid ID to claim your birthday gifts.

Here are the free gifts:

- Free beauty gift from Sephora ($15)
- Free beauty gift from Ulta rewards
- Go to Build-a-Bear on a child's birthday and you pay your age for the bear! Great way to save $20 if you're travelling with kids.

And here's where you can sample a free meal, birthday treat or heavy discount:

- Capital Grille – get free dessert with your meal!
- Baskin Robbins – a free scoop!
- Sprinkles Cupcakes – a free birthday cupcake!
- Panera – a free pastry!
- Starbucks Coffee - show your loyalty card and get a free coffee
- Jamba Juice - free juice.
- List of New York Birthday Freebies
- Anthony's Coal Fired Pizza - a FREE 12" Pizza.
- IKEA - FREE restaurant meal + $15 store gift certificate.
- Krispy Kreme free dozen donuts.

Here is a regularly updated list of NYC Birthday freebies: https://www.favoritecandle.com/free-birthday-meals/New-York/NY

Key dates

January - Martin Luther King Jr Day Every year on the third Monday of January a parade between 61st and 86th St. on 5th Avenue commemorates the famous civil rights activist.

March - St Patrick's Day Parade New York is famous for its St Patrick's Day parade which is the world's largest outside Ireland. Book your spot on Fifth Ave for the best view.

April - Tartan Day Parade Over 10,000 pipers and drummers congregate on 6th Ave to celebrate their Scottish roots for this annual parade.

May - Ninth Avenue Food Festival Just two blocks west of Times Square in Hell's Kitchen, this food festival attracts a million people who come to sample culinary delights from all over the world.

June - Museum Mile Festival For one day in June NYC's Museum Mile becomes one big block party. There's live music and lots more.

July - Independence Day On July 4th a huge fireworks display takes place over the East River. To make sure you witness it, you just have to make sure you get a spot close to the river!

August - Blues, Barbecue and Fireworks Festival Enjoy free music, barbecued food and a huge fireworks display at this one-day festival as part of the Hudson River Park's 'Summer of Fun'.

September - San Gennaro Festival Little Italy becomes awash with activity for this annual festival which takes place on Mulberry St. Sample various culinary delights, and if you're not hungry, play various games at different stalls.

October - Oktoberfest Munich isn't the only city where Oktoberfest is celebrated - New York gets in on the act also! Third Ave closes and drinking, eating, dancing, and everything German is celebrated.

November - Macy's Thanksgiving Day Parade This huge parade is one of the biggest events of the year as massive balloons and floats make their way down 7th Ave.

December - Grand Central Laser Light Show A spectacular light show is beamed on to the ceiling on New York's central train station for 6 weeks at the end of every year.

Where to stay?

This is a personal preference and should be based on your interests and what attractions you plan to visit in the city. Midtown East (near Grand Central Terminal) is good for exploring the city. The best price/ performance ratio is East Williamsburg.

Long Island City is good if you want great **views of the Manhattan skyline** – just not too far to the east of Long Island, places like Montauk and the Hamptons are not budget.

Areas to avoid
DO NOT STAY OUTSIDE of the city. You will be reliant on the train schedule and round-trip tickets to Grand Central were $25 per person during peak hours ($20 off-peak). When traveling with a group, the price of train tickets can add up and you will be better off using that money towards a room in the city.

The cheapest place to stay
If you're travelling solo hostels are your best option in New York, both for meeting people and saving pennies. Well-reviewed   is conveniently located in East Williamsburg and they offer dorms from $20. We stayed in an Airbnb as we were two so it was cheaper - and we took the transit bus in to the city. Airbnbs are expensive in New York but work out cheaper if you are travelling as a group.

Local Discount Accommodation

Aside from Booking and Airbnb you can find discount b and b's on this site: https://www.cozycozy.com/us/manhattan-bed-and-breakfast

Hack your New York Accommodation

Your two biggest expenses when travelling to New York are accommodation and food. This section is intended to help you cut these costs dramatically before and while you are in New York.

Hostels are the cheapest accommodation in New York but there are some creative workarounds to upgrade your stay on the cheap.

Use Time

There are two ways to use time. One is to book in advance. Three months will net you the best deal, especially if your visit coincides with an event. The other is to book on the day of your stay. This is a risky move, but if executed well, you can lay your head in a five-star hotel for a 2-star fee.

Before you travel to New York, checked for big events using a simple google search 'What's on in New York', if you find no big events drawing travellers, risk showing up with no accommodation booked (If there are big events on demand exceeds supply and you should avoid using this strategy). Start checking for discount rooms at 11 am using a private browser on booking.com.

Before I go into demand-based pricing, take a moment to think about your risk tolerance. By risk, I am not talking about personal safety. No amount of financial savings is worth risking that. What I am talking about is being inconvenienced. Do you deal well with last-minute changes? Can you roll with the punches or do you freak out if something changes? Everyone is different and knowing yourself is the best way to plan a great trip. If you are someone that likes to have everything pre-planned using demand-based pricing to get cheap accommodation will not work for you. Skip this section and go to blind-booking.

Demand-based pricing

Be they an Airbnb host or hotel manager; no one wants empty rooms. Most will do anything to make some revenue because they still have the same costs to cover whether the room is occupied or not. That's why you will find many hotels drastically slashing room rates for same-day bookings.

How to book five-star hotels for a two-star price

You will not be able to find these discounts when the demand exceeds the supply. So if you're visiting during the peak season, or during an event which has drawn many travellers again don't try this.

On the day of your stay, visit booking.com (which offers better discounts than Kayak and agoda.com). Hotel Tonight individually checks for any last-minute bookings, but they take a big chunk of the action, so the better deals come from booking.com. The best results come from booking between 2 pm and 4 pm when the risk of losing any revenue with no occupancy is most pronounced, so algorithms supporting hotels slash prices. This is when you can find rates that are not within the "lowest publicly visible" rate. To avoid losing customers to other websites, or cheapening the image of their hotel most will only offer the super cheap rates during a two hour window from 2 pm to 4 pm. Two guests will pay 10x difference in price but it's absolutely vital to the hotel that neither knows it.

Takeaway: To get the lowest price book on the day of stay between 2 pm and 4 pm and extend your search radius to include further afield hotels with good transport connections.

Priceline Hack to get a Luxury Hotel on the Cheap

Priceline.com has been around since 1997 and is an incredible site for sourcing luxury Hotels on the cheap in New York. If you've tried everything else and that's failed, priceline will deliver.

Priceline have a database of the lowest price a hotel will accept for a particular time and date. That amount changes depending on two factors:

1. Demand: More demand high prices.
2. Likelihood of lost revenue: if the room is still available at 3pm the same-day prices will plummet.

Obviously they don't want you to know the lowest price as they make more commission the higher the price you pay.

They offer two good deals to entice you to book with them in New York. **And the good news is neither require last-minute booking (though the price will decrease the closer to the date you book).**

'Firstly, 'price-breakers'. You blind book from a choice of three highly rated hotels which they name. Pricebreakers, travelers are shown three similar, highly-rated hotels, listed under a single low price.' After you book they reveal the name of the hotel.

Secondly, the 'express deals'. These are the last minute deals. You'll be able to see the name of the hotel before you book.

To find the right luxury hotel for you at a cheap price you should plug in the
neighbourhoods you want to stay in, an acceptable rating (4 or 5 stars), and filter by the amenities you want.

You can also get an addition discount for your New York hotel by booking on their dedicated app.

How to trick travel Algorithms to get the lowest hotel price

Do not believe anyone who says changing your IP address to get cheaper hotels or flights does NOT work. If you don't believe us, download a Tor Network and search for flights and hotels to one destination using your current IP and then the tor network (a tor browser hides your IP address from algorithms. It is commonly used by hackers). You will receive different prices.

The price you see is a decision made by an algorithm that adjusts prices using data points such as past bookings, remaining capacity, average demand and the probability of selling the room or flight later at a higher price. If knows you've searched for the area before ip the prices high. To circumvent this, you can either use a different IP address from a cafe or airport or data from an international sim. I use a sim from Three, which provides free data in many countries around the world. When you search from a new IP address, most of the time, and particularly near booking you will get a lower price. Sometimes if your sim comes from a 'rich' country, say the UK or USA, you will see higher rates as the algorithm has learnt people from these countries pay more. The solution is to book from a local wifi connection - but a different one from the one you originally searched from.

How to get last-minute discounts on owner rented properties

In addition to Airbnb, you can also find owner rented rooms and apartments on www.vrbo.com or HomeAway or a host of others.

Nearly all owners renting accommodation will happily give renters a "last-minute" discount to avoid the space sitting empty, not earning a dime.

Go to Airbnb or another platform and put in today's date. Once you've found something you like start the negotiating by asking for a 25% reduction. A sample message to an Airbnb host might read:

Dear HOST NAME,

I love your apartment. It looks perfect for me. Unfortunately, I'm on a very tight budget. I hope you won't be offended, but I wanted to ask if you would be amenable to offering me a 25% discount for tonight, tomorrow and the following day? I see that you aren't booked. I can assure you, I will leave your place exactly the way I found it. I will put bed linen in the washer and ensure everything is clean for the next guest. I would be delighted to bring you a bottle of wine to thank you for any discount that you could offer.

If this sounds okay, please send me a custom offer, and I will book straight away.

YOUR NAME.

In my experience, a polite, genuine message like this, that proposes reciprocity will be successful 80% of the time. Don't ask for more than 25% off, this person still has to pay the bills and will probably say no as your stay will cost them more in bills than they make. Plus starting higher, can offend the owner and do you want to stay somewhere, where you have offended the host?

In Practice

To use either of these methods, you must travel light. Less stuff means greater mobility, everything is faster and you don't have to check-in or store luggage. If you have a lot of luggage, you're going to have fewer of these opportunities to save on accommodation. Plus travelling light benefits the planet - you're buying, consuming, and transporting less stuff.

Blind-booking

If your risk tolerance does not allow for last-minute booking, you can use blind-booking. Many hotels not wanting to cheapen their brand with known low-prices, choose to operate a blind booking policy. This is where you book without knowing the name of the hotel you're going to stay in until you've made the payment. This is also sometimes used as a marketing strategy where the hotel is seeking to recover from past issues. I've stayed in plenty of blind book hotels. As long as you choose 4 or 5 star hotels, you will find them to be clean, comfortable and safe. priceline.com, Hot Rate® Hotels and Top Secret Hotels (operated by last-minute.com) offer the best deals.

Hotels.com Loyalty Program

This is currently the best hotel loyalty program with hotels in New York. The basic premise is you collect 10 nights and get 1 free. hotels.com price match, so if booking.com has a cheaper price you can get hotel.com, to match. If you intend to travel more than ten nights in a year, its a great choice to get the 11th free.

Don't let time use you.

Rigidity will cost you money. You pay the price you're willing to pay, not the amount it requires a hotel to deliver. Therefore if you're in town for a big event, saving money on accommodation is nearly impossible so in such cases book three months ahead.

The best price performance location in New York

A room putting New York attractions, restaurants, and nightlife within walking distance will save you time on transport. However restaurants and bars don't get that much cheaper the further you go from famous tourist attractions. But you will also get a better idea of the day to day life of a local if you stay in a neighbourhood like East Williamsburg. It depends on the New York you want to experience. For the tourist experience stay in the centre either in a last-minute hotel or Airbnb. For a taste of local life the urban cool district of East Williamsburg is the best you will find. Groupon, Roomorama and Living Social. Both offer significant deals on New York City hotels.

What to do if you only find over-priced options

If when you're searching for accommodation, you can only find overpriced offers, it's likely that you're visiting at a time where demand outstrips supply. In this case, have a look at www.trustedhousesitters.com. You stay for free when you care for someones pets. If you really can't find a good deal, this can be worth doing but only you know if you want to make a commitment to care for someone else's pets while on vacation. Some find it relaxing, others don't. The properties in New York can be even more stunning than five-star hotels but if you're new to house sitting you might be against 10+ applicants, so make sure your profile is really strong before you apply for a sit. It could save you a small fortune and, who knows, you could even make some new (furry and non-furry) friends.

How to be a green tourist in New York

New York like other major cities struggles with high levels of air pollution. The city suffered years of severe smog, with instances like the harming thousands of residents. Thankfully the and local legislation has provided for much needed improvements. Still its important as responsible tourists that we help not hinder New York. There is a bizarre misconception that you have to spend money to travel in an eco-friendly way. This like, all marketing myths was concocted and hyped by companies seeking to make money off of you. In my experience, anything with eco in front of their names e.g Eco-tours will be triple the cost of the regular tour. Don't get me wrong sometimes its best to take these tours if you're visiting endangered areas, but normally such places have extensive legislation that everyone, including the eco and non-eco tour companies must comply with. The vast majority of ways you can travel eco-friendly are free and even save you money:

- Avoid Bottled Water - get a good water bottle and refill. The water in New York is safe to drink.

- Thrift shop but check the labels and don't buy polyester clothes - overtime plastic is released into the ocean when we wash polyester.

- Don't put your shopping in a plastic bag, bring a cotton tote with you when you venture out.

- Pack Light - this is one of the best ways to save money. If you find a 5-star hotel for tonight for $10, and you're at an Airbnb or hostel, you can easily pack and upgrade hassle-free. A light pack equals freedom and it means less to wash.

- Travel around New York on Bikes or e-Scooters or use Public Transportation. Car Pool with services like bla bla car or Uber/Lyft share.

- Walk, this is the best way to get to know New York. You never know what's around the corner.

Saving money on New York Food

Use 'Too Good To Go'

New York offers plenty of food bargains; if you know where to look. Thankfully the app 'Too Good to Go' is turning visitors into locals by showing them exactly where to find the tastiest deals and simultaneously rescue food that would otherwise be wasted. In New York you can pick up a $15 buy of baked goods, groceries, breakfast, brunch, lunch or dinner boxes for $2.99. You'll find lots of fish and meat dishes on offer in New York, which would normally be expensive.

How it works? You pay for a magic bag (essentially a bag of what the restaurant or bakery has leftover) on the app and simply pick it up from the bakery or restaurant during the time they've selected. You can find extremely cheap breakfast, lunch, dinner and even groceries this way. Simply download the app and press 'my current location' to find the deals near you in New York. What's not to love about delicious food thats a quarter of the normal price and helping to drive down food waste?

An oft-quoted parable is 'There is no such thing as cheap food. Either you pay at the cash registry or the doctor's office'. This dismisses the fact that good nutrition is a choice; we all make every-time we eat. Cheap eats are not confined to hotdogs and kebabs. The great thing about using Too Good To Go is you can eat nutritious food cheaply: fruits, vegetables, fish and nut dishes are a fraction of their supermarket cost.

Japan has the longest life expectancy in the world. A national study by the Japanese Ministry of Internal Affairs and Communications revealed that between January and May 2019, a household of two spent on average ¥65,994 a month, that's $10 per person per day on food. You truly don't need to spend a lot to eat nutritious food. That's a marketing gimmick hawkers of overpriced muesli bars want you to believe.

Check out this local Facebook group (https://www.facebook.com/groups/471563341060101/) where people share pictures of the food they picked up from restaurants and supermarkets in New York. It's a great way to see what's on offer and find food you'll love.

Our favourite magic bags in New York come from Der Pioneer and Windsor Terrace. Never pick up a bag with a rating lower than 4.2 on the Too Good To Go app. People using it tend to be kinder because its fighting food waster. PLEASE don't waste your time on places with a rating below 4.2.

Hit the oyster happy hours
Love oysters? Go to an Oyster Happy Hour at Jeffery's Grocery, The Dead Rabbit, upstate craft beer & oyster bar, Sel Rrose or Crave Fishbar. Many of the places mentioned offer $2 oysters weekdays from 4 p.m. to 7 p.m.

Don't eat Italian food in Little Venice
Though the food is excellent, the prices are touristy prices. Instead head to Arthur Avenue in the Bronx for authentic Italian restaurants at less than half the price of those in Little Venice.

Breakfast
If you stay somewhere with a free breakfast, eat smart. Don't eat sugary cereals or white flour rich pastries if you

don't want to be hungry an hour later. Before leaving your hotel or checking out, find some fresh fruit, water, and granola in the fitness centre or coffee in the lobby or business centre. If your hotel doesn't have free breakfast, don't take it. You can always eat cheaper outside.

Johny's Luncheonette has the best cheap breakfast we found. Here you can pick up pancakes for less than $3.

Visit supermarkets at discount times.

You can get a 50 per cent discount around 5 pm at the Whole Foods supermarkets on fresh produce. The cheaper the supermarket, the less discounts you will find, so check Whole Foods supermarkets at 5 pm before the discount supermarkets. Some items are also marked down due to sell-by date after the lunchtime rush so its also worth to check in around 3 pm.

Go to BYOB restaurants

Many restaurants don't have alcohol licenses but let you bring your own drinks. Sine one beer can easily cost $10, you can save a lot of money. If you love to drink while you dine, check out Lucali · Tartine · Spicy Village · Peking Duck House · Panna II Garden · Tanoshi Sushi NYC · Wondee Siam or Astoria.

Use delivery services on the cheap.

Take advantage of local offers on food delivery services. Many of the newest ones are flush with Venture Capital Money and hence are offering major discounts for new customers. These include GoPuff, FridgeNoMore and Gorilla.

Most established platforms including Seamless and Door Dash offer $10 off the first order in New York.

SNAPSHOT: How to enjoy a $5,000 trip to New York for $350

(full breakdown at the end of the guide)

Stay	Travelling in peak season: 1. Last-minute hotels via priceline.com express deals 2. Stay in a private room in a Airbnb if you want privacy and cooking facilities. 3. Stay in hostels if you want to meet over travellers. 4. University accommodation in summer time 5. Housesit. 6. Nap York - $20 a night sleep pod. Travelling in low season 1. Last minute five-star hotels. You can find Private room on airbnb for $22 a night in the city. Here is the link to a perfect https://www.airbnb.com/rooms/653612940490299787 If you're visiting during vacation times look at student dorm rooms - https://www.universityrooms.com/en-GB/city/newyork/home/
Eat	From bagels to corned-beef sandwiches, Italian fine dining to curbside fast food, and from sashimi to sauerkraut, the breadth of cuisines is matched only by the range of prices. But you don't have to spend huge amounts to eat well. Budget an average of $5 - $15 for each meal.
Move	Use the Subway. It costs $32 for a weeks unlimited travel.
See	Free museums, Staten Island Ferry, a Broadway show, markets, street art and so much more. totalling $20 in entrance fees when you follow our tips on how to visit free or cheap)
Experience	Michelin-star restaurants, rooftop bars and broadway.
Total	US$350

Unique bargains I love in New York

New York has the reputation of being among the most luxurious and expensive destinations in the world. Fortunately, some of the best things in life are free (or almost free). There are a plethora of amazing free tours, free concerts, cheap theatre and film screenings, pay-what-you-wish nights at museums, city festivals, plus loads of green space to escape the urban sprawl.

Chelsea market and Gotham Food Hall are great for cheap eats. Also, it's always a good idea to picnic in Washington square park and Central Park (really any park). Murray's Cheese shop is near Washington square and you could get delicious grilled cheese or cheese/meat plate and bread and wine to take to the park - it makes for a lovely afternoon. Plus there are usually free shows in Bryant park and Central Park.

The first thing you should do when you arrive is check https://www.timeout.com/newyork/things-to-do/things-to-do-in-new-york-today to see what free events are on. Many entice people to come with free food and drink. Even the most reluctant bargain hunter can be successful in New York..

Take your student card

New York offers hundreds of student discounts. If you're studying buy an ISIC card - International Student Identity Card. It's a great investment because its valid in 133 countries and covers 150,000 discounts including many hundreds in New York.

Senior discounts

Nearly every major museum, attraction and The MTA offers reduced fares for seniors age 65.

How to use this book

Google and TripAdvisor are your on-the-go guides while traveling, a travel guide adds the most value during the planning phase, and if you're without Wi-Fi. Always download the google map for your destination - having an offline map will make using this guide much more comfortable. For ease of use, we've set the book out the way you travel, booking your flights, arriving, how to get around, then on to the money-saving tips. The tips we ordered according to when you need to know the tip to save money, so free tours and combination tickets feature first. We prioritized the rest of the tips by how much money you can save and then by how likely it was that you could find the tip with a google search. Meaning those we think you could find alone are nearer the bottom. I hope you find this layout useful. If you have any ideas about making Super Cheap Insider Guides easier to use, please email me philgattang@gmail.com

A quick note on How We Source Super Cheap Tips
We focus entirely on finding the best bargains. We give each of our collaborators $2,000 to hunt down never-before-seen deals. The type you either only know if you're local or by on the ground research. We spend zero on marketing and a little on designing an excellent cover. We do this yearly, which means we just keep finding more amazing ways for you to have the same experience for less.

Now let's get started with juicing the most pleasure from your trip to New York with the least possible money!

OUR SUPER CHEAP TIPS...

Here are out specific tips to enjoy a $5,000 trip to New York for $350

How to Find Super Cheap Flights to New York

Luck is just an illusion. Anyone can find incredible flight deals. If you can be flexible you can save huge amounts of money. In fact, the biggest tip I can give you for finding incredible flight deals is simple: find a flexible job. Don't despair if you can't do that theres still a lot you can do. The following pages detail the exact method I use to consistently find cheap flights to New York.

Book your flight to New York on a Tuesday or Wednesday

Tuesdays and Wednesdays are the cheapest days of the week to fly. You can take a flight to New York on a Tuesday or Wednesday for less than half the price you'd pay on a Thursday Friday, Saturday, Sunday or Monday.

Start with Google Flights (but NEVER book through them)

I conduct upwards of 50 flight searches a day for readers. I use google flights first when looking for flights. I put specific departure but broad destination (e.g Europe) and usually find amazing deals.

The great thing about Google Flights is you can search by class. You can pick a specific destination and it will tell you which time is cheapest in which class. Or you can put in dates and you can see which area is cheapest to travel to.

But be aware Google flights does not show the cheapest prices among the flight search engines but it does offer several advantages

1. You can see the cheapest dates for the next 8 weeks. Other search engines will blackout over 70% of the prices.
2. You can put in multiple airports to fly from. Just use a common to separate in the from input.
3. If you're flexible on where you're going Google flights can show you the cheapest destinations.
4. You can set-up price tracking, where Google will email you when prices rise or decline.

Once you have established the cheapest dates to fly go over to skyscanner.net and put those dates in. You will find sky scanner offers the cheapest flights.

Get Alerts when Prices to New York are Lowest

Google also has a nice feature which allows you to set up an alert to email you when prices to your destination are at their lowest. So if you don't have fixed dates this feature can save you a fortune.

Baggage add-ons

It may be cheaper and more convenient to send your luggage separately with a service like sendmybag.com Often the luggage sending fee is cheaper than what the airlines charge to check baggage. Visit Lugless.com or luggagefree.com in addition to sendmybag.com for a quotation.

Loading times

Anyone who has attempted to find a cheap flight will know the pain of excruciating long loading times. If you encounter this issue use google flights to find the cheapest dates and then go to skyscanner.net for the lowest price.

Always try to book direct with the airline

Once you have found the cheapest flight go direct to the airlines booking page. This is advantageous in the current covid cancellation climate, because if you need to change your flights or arrange a refund, its much easier to do so, than via a third party booking agent.

That said, sometimes the third party bookers offer cheaper deals than the airline, so you need to make the decision based on how likely you think it is that disruption will impede you making those flights.

More flight tricks and tips

www.secretflying.com/usa-deals offers a range of deals from the USA and other countries. For example you can pick-up a round trip flight non-stop from from the east coast to johannesburg for $350 return on this site

Scott's cheap flights, you can select your home airport and get emails on deals but you pay for an annual subscription. A free workaround is to download Hopper and set search alerts for trips/ price drops.

Premium service of Scott's cheap flights.
They sometime have discounted business and first class but in my experience they are few and far between.

JGOOT.com has 5 times as many choices as Scott's cheap flights.

kiwi.com allows you to be able to do radius searches so you can find cheaper flights to general areas.

Finding Error Fares
Travel Pirates (www.travelpirates.com) is a gold-mine for finding error deals. Subscribe to their newsletter. I recently found a reader an airfare from Montreal-Brazil for a $200 round trip (mistake fare!). Of course these error fares are always certain dates, but if you can be flexible you can save a lot of money.

Things you can do that might reduce the fare to New York:--
- Use a VPN (if the booker knows you booked one-way, the return fare will go up)
- Buy your ticket in a different currency

How to Find CHEAP FIRST-CLASS Flights to New York

Upgrade at the airport

Airlines are extremely reluctant to advertise price drops in first or business class tickets so the best way to secure them is actually at the airport when airlines have no choice but to decrease prices dramatically because otherwise they lose money. Ask about upgrading to business or first-class when you check-in. If you check-in online look around the airport for your airlines branded bidding system. For example KLM at Amsterdam have terminals where you can bid on upgrades.

Use Air-miles

When it comes to accruing air-miles for American citizens **Chase Sapphire Reserve card** ranks top. If you put everything on there and pay it off immediately you will end up getting free flights all the time, aside from taxes.

Get 2-3 chase cards with sign up bonuses, you'll have 200k points in no time and can book with points on multiple airlines when transferring your points to them.

Please note, this is only applicable to those living in the USA. In the Bonus Section we have detailed the best air-mile credit cards for those living in the UK, Canada, Germany, Austria, Spain and Australia.

How many miles does it take to fly first class?

First class from Bangkok to Chicago (one way) costs 180,000 miles.

Cheapest route to NYC from Europe

At the time of writing Norwegian are flying to New York for around $260 return from Paris.

Arriving

There are three airports in New York and the cheapest way to and from them all is with public transport.

Here's the cheapest method from each airport:

From Newark: The trains from Newark costs $15.50 per person to Manhattan.

From LGA you can take M60 bus from all terminals at La-Guardia airport bus to 125th street in Manhattan for $3.75.

From JFK you'll have to take the airtrain to get on the sub-way system. Then the subway to your destination. One way $10.

Take a helicopter from the airport to Manhattan

If you're landing at JFK and want the ultimate bougie arrival into Manhattan you can take a helicopter from JKF into Manhattan. blade.com are offering the flight for $195 plus you'll receive three free drinks and obviously a helicopter ride over Manhattan. The average 15-minute ride over Mahanttan is approximately $235 making this a steal. And here's the super cheap part, they are offering 50% discounts. Either use a plugin like 'HONEY' to find a code or google discount code for Blade. This is the last code I found to be working in November 2022 - MATTHEWC002

Need a place to store luggage?
Use stasher.com to find a convenient place to store your luggage cheaply. It provides much cheaper options than airport and train station lockers in New York.

Getting around

New York City is composed of five boroughs: The Bronx, Brooklyn, Manhattan, Queens, and Staten Island. Brooklyn has the largest population at 2.5 million.

E-scooters/ bike sharing
Like a growing number of cities around the world, New York has a bike-sharing program - . A single ride is $3 or a day pass is $12.

Public transport
Get an unlimited MTA weekly card - $33 - to use the subway. It's the cheapest and easiest way to get around the city. The first underground line of the subway opened on October 27, 1904, Though the city's first official subway line was the IRT, which opened in 1868.

Tips for Riding the New York City Subway
Tips for Riding the New York City Subway

- Check MTA.info for Delays and Detours.
- Avoid Rush Hour 7am to 10am and 4pm to 7pm.
- Use a Metrocard.
- Use the Free Subway to Bus Transfers.
- Before you board check if a Train is Going Uptown or
- Downtown.
- Pickpockets target tourists in New York. Disguise yourself
- as a local by buying a local branded reusable supermarket
- bag to use as your day bag.

The NYC subway is quite dirty due to the vacuum trains the MTA uses to suck up trash, which they bought in 1997 and 2000, frequently don't run when they're supposed to because they are broken down so often.

INSIDER CULTURAL INSIGHT

As you sit on the subway imagine that one day they will be submerged under the Ocean. As of 2019 2,500 decommissioned subway carriages have been sunk to provide habitats for sea creatures.

Take the ferry
'There are six routes, as well as one seasonal route, connecting 25 ferry piers across all five boroughs. The longest line from the NYC Ferry is: RW. This Ferry route starts from Rockaway (Queens) and ends at Wall St/Pier 11 (Manhattan). It covers over 25 km and has 3 stops." Tickets are $2.75.

Get around for FREE
Use ride sharing service Lyft. Google for a free credit and open a new Lyft account. New York offers up to $50 free credit, which could cover your transport for your whole trip.

Walk – it's the best way to discover New York. Take a different route, and you just might see the City from a whole new angle.

Use public transportation to avoid the hefty cab prices. Take the AirTrain, the airport's public transit line to connect with New York City's subways, buses, and rails. Public transportation is the most affordable way to get to downtown and may be the fastest with traffic.

INSIDER CULTURAL INSIGHT

Manhattan's name originates from its a native history: Man-nahata, or 'island of many hills' in the native Lenape lan-guage.

Drive - there's an app called 'Getaround' which allows you to rent a car from $0.19 per minute + more for the Kilome-tre's but it's cheaper than a car rental and you can do hourly, daily or even weekly packages. You just scan the QR code on the code, hop in and drive.

Orientate yourself with this free tour

Forget exploring New York by wandering around aimlessly. Always start with a free organised tour if one is available. Nothing compares to local advice, especially when travelling on a budget. I gleamed many of our super cheap tips from local guides and locals in general, so start with a organised tour to get your bearings and ask for their recommendations for the best cheap eats, the best bargains, the best markets, the best place for a particular street eat. Perhaps some of it will be repeated from this guide, but it can't hurt to ask, especially if you have specific needs or questions. At the end you should leave an appropriate tip (usually around $5), but nobody bats an eye lid if you are unable or unwilling to do so, tell them you will leave a good review and always give them a little gift from home - I always carry small Vienna fridge magnets and I always tip the $5, but it is totally up to you.

The best free tour is with the greeters - locals who show you NYC. You can choose the neighborhood you want to tour, just book here: www.bigapplegreeter.org Reserve at least four weeks in advance to avoid disappointment.

There are 19 more free Tours available including Central Park. Lower Manhattan. 9/11 Memorial and World Trade Center. Greenwich Village. Food Tour of Greenwich Village. SoHo. The Brooklyn Bridge and The High Line:

INSIDER HISTORICAL INSIGHT
Standard street signs are green, look out for brown signs they indicate historic districts.

INSIDER MONEY SAVING TIP

If you have more time consider Geocaching. This is where you hunt for hide-and-seek containers. You need a mobile device to follow the GPS clues in New York. A typical cache is a small, waterproof container with a logbook where you can leave a message or see various trinkets left by other cache hunters. Build your own treasure hunt by discovering geocaches in New York.

Consider the New York Pass

If you plan to hit all the major attractions in New York the New York pass can save you money on: Top of the Rock, Empire State Building, 9/11 Memorial Museum and 97 more attractions. Starting at $150 for adults for one day it is not cheap. However if you got up early to do the top attractions it works out at $19 per attraction. The key benefit is as well as saving money, you save time on queuing.

Buy the pass online and save 30% off the retail price. You can download the New York Pass mobile ticket. Consult the website to see if it matches your needs

If you're travelling with kids

- Washington Square Park has amazing playgrounds for toddlers and older children.
- Bryant Park puts on juggling lessons, free theatre and puppet shows.
- Brooklyn Bridge Park has (as mentioned) free kayaking in the summer and SPARK Children's Museum free on Thursdays from 1 pm - 6 pm.
- There is also the historic Jane's Carousel. Though the carousel does cost $2,
- Hudson River Park has many free activities for kids.
- SeaGlass Carousel in Battery park is only $5.50.

Visit these incredible Free Museums

To make sure everybody has access to culture many of New York's top museums are free or have times when you can visit for free. Here are the best of the crop:

These museums are Always Free
National Museum of the American Indian - part of the Smithsonian Institution and is committed to advancing knowledge and understanding of the Native cultures of the Western Hemisphere—past, present, and future—through partnership with Native people and others

National September 11 Memorial

Museum at FIT - collection of garments & accessories

Hamilton Grange - preserves the relocated home of U.S. Founding Father Alexander Hamilton
American Folk Art Museum
Nicholas Roerich Museum Admission by Donation
American Museum of Natural History
Brooklyn Museum
Museum of the City of New York
Brooklyn Historical Society - Free or Pay-What-You-Wish on Certain Days
The Queens Museum is also free (need to book a timed entry though). Corona Park is site of 1962 World's Fair and the museum is one of the fair "leftovers". The diorama and art exhibits are cool.

These museums are Free at selected times:

MoMA – 4–9pm Friday
MET - FREE every Friday from 4 pm-8 pm
Rubin Museum of Art – 6–10pm Friday
Asia Society & Museum – 6–9pm Friday, September to June Japan Society – 6–9pm Friday
Frick Collection – 2–6pm Wednesday & 6–9pm first Friday of month
New Museum of Contemporary Art – 7–9pm Thursday
New-York Historical Society – 6–8pm Friday
Jewish Museum – 5–8pm Thursday and Saturday
Guggenheim Museum – 5:45–7:45pm Saturday -
Take the elevator to the top floor of the Guggenheim and m ake your way down the spiral
ramp, taking in highlights of 20th
century art along the way.
Whitney Museum of American Art – 7–10pm Friday Neue Galerie – 6–8pm first Friday of month

Museum of Natural History is free for the last hour of every day

Visit NYC's Top Free Historical Sights

- Ellis Island (New York Harbor)
  - Gracie Mansion (Upper East Side)
  - Merchant's House Museum (NoHo)
  - Jane's Carousel (Brooklyn)
  - Historic Richmond Town (Staten Island)

FREE TOUR ALERT: Cooper Hewitt Smithsonian Design Museum offers Free tours are at 11:30am and 1:30pm on weekdays, and at 1pm and 3pm on weekends.

Go to a Broadway show on the cheap

The origins of Broadway history in New York begun in 1750 when a theater company was opened on Nassau Street. This theater was large enough to hold 280 people and mainly put on Shakespearian plays and ballad operas. Over three centuries later over 15 million people flock to see broadway shows. With the average ticket price costing $124, its not cheap. Luckily there are eight ways for you to buy super cheap tickets.

By buying your tickets on the day of the show you can get them 50% cheaper. There are two ways to do this:

1. Download the Today Tix app
2. Go to the TKTS booth right in Times Square that opens twice a day and sells cheap broadway shows for that day. The big shows like Wicked and Book of Mormon won't have but you can find good seats for other major performances from $15.

3. Many shows also offer rush tickets (Most productions hold back a percentage of tickets to sell on the day) as online digital lotteries now, where you enter the day or two before and hope for the best. Here's a list: https://www.playbill.com/article/broadway-rush-lottery-and-standing-room-only-policies-com-116003
4. Rush tickets at the box office. Show up at the productions box office 10am on Monday to Saturday and noon on Sundays to get deeply discounted 'rush tickets'.
5. 'Not all Broadway shows offer Standing Room Only tickets, but for the ones that do, the average cost of these deeply discounted tickets is about $25' Tickets Are Usually For Sold-Out Performances Only. Here's a list of shows which offer standing tickets - https://www.nytix.com/discount-broadway-tickets

If same-day tickets don't suit you there are other options.

1. If you're open to any show, try Broadway Roulette. You pick the day, it picks the show. You can get major productions from $25.
2. Broadway For Broke People has options the day ahead of when you want to go to a Broadway show.
3. The Will-Call Club is a theater seat filling service that offers discount tickets* to Broadway. You pay $20 for a yearly membership. It's probably worth the fee if you're in the US for a longer time.

Eat at a Cheap Michelin starred restaurant

Tribeca is home to a few one-starred Michelin restaurants. Bâtard is one of the best, this French–Italian Michelin starred restaurant has a BYOB on Mondays. Its very reasonable priced for a Michelin starred restaurant and if you go on Monday you don't need to pay for drinks because you can bring your own. Make reservations ahead of time:
https://www.batardtribeca.com/

Do free wine tastings

'The Finger Lakes area is the main New York wine region for the production of Riesling, Long Island and Hamptons area are known for their Merlot and Cabernet Franc.' Thanks to the variety of nearby vineyards there are lots of shops which offer free wine tastings. Here are the best:

- September Wines - in the Lower East Side
- Chelsea Wine Vault in the Chelsea Market
- Union Square Wines in Union Square
- Nolita Wine Merchants - near Little Italy
- Astor Wines in the East Village

Walk The High Line

The High Line was a freight rail line, in operation from 1934 to 1980. Today it is an elevated linear park, greenway and rail trail created on a former New York Central Railroad. It provides some of the best views of the city and is great for snapping photos. You start at Gansevoort Street in the Meatpacking District and end at West 34th Street, between 10th and 12th Avenues.

Take the FREE Staten Island Ferry

The best way to see The Statue of Liberty is with the 25 minute FREE ride on the Staten Island ferry. Leaving from South Ferry Terminal in Lower Manhattan, on it you can enjoy breathtaking views of Lower Manhattan's skyline and an even better one of the Statue of Liberty. Be aware of scammers trying to sell tickets, the ferry is free.
From May to October, you can also take a FREE ferry over to Governors Island, a car-free island with great views. For more adventure, take out a free kayak, available in the Hudson River Park,
Brooklyn Bridge Park and Red Hook.

Visit this Cheap alternative to the Empire State Building

This famous art-deco skyscraper opened in 1930, it is no longer New York's tallest building but it has one of the best sunset views. Plus the newly added LED lights create more than 16 million color possibilities. If you go up to the top it will costs you $39. The best time to visit is sunset.

If you don't want to pay the $39 for the view, head to The Spyglass Rooftop Bar. The view from top is unmatched in New York. It is not the highest, but it is an intimate view and quite lovely. Plus, no one really goes there anymore so it's not touristy and it will cost you the price of a soda.

Walk across the Brooklyn Bridge

Brooklyn Bridge is a suspension/cable-stay
hybrid bridge connecting Manhattan and Brooklyn. It is one
of the oldest suspension bridges in United States (complet-
ed in 1883) and a first steel-wire suspension bridge in the
world.Jump on a 4, 5 or 6 train to Brooklyn Bridge. You will
be at the Manhattan end of New York's most famous bridge.
Afterwards take a break in the Empire Fulton Ferry State
Park on the Brooklyn side.

Go to a top TV show for free

Fancy being in the audience of famous TV shows? Many are taped in New York City Including: The Late Show with Stephen Colbert, The Drew Barrymore Show, The Daily Show with Trevor Noah and The Tonight Show Starring Jimmy Fallon give out free audience tickets. Either go to TKTS booth in Times Square on Mondays or Tuesdays and you should find somebody heckling about free tickets or log on to https://www.tvtaping.com/ to reserve your spot. https://www.nycgo.com/articles/live-tv-show-tapings-and-tickets also posts calls for audience members.

Take in breathtaking Tram Views

Roosevelt Island Aerial Tram costs about $6 return and a free bus takes you around Roosevelt. The jaw-dropping 360-degree view of New York City is best enjoyed at night and the tram runs past midnight every night.

If you'd like to see another breathtaking night view of New York take the East River Ferry just $2.75. It runs past 9 pm every night.

Do some free high-powered Stargazing

From April to October, members of the Amateur Astronomers Association bring high-powered telescopes to various parks in NYC. For times and parks visit: https://www.aosny.org/

Visit New York Public Library

Built in 1911, it is the largest marble structure ever built in the United States. The New York Public Library is monumental and gorgeous inside. It is also an awesome place to go if you are looking for a quiet to escape NYC's crazy. My favourite place to read is the Rose Reading Room on the 3rd floor. There's also free wifi and charging sockets.

Go to The Bronx Zoo for FREE!

The Bronx Zoo opened its doors to the public in 1899. It is home to over 4,000 animals. **Wednesday's are free at the Bronx Zoo**, they do ask you to consider making a donation to help in caring for the 600 species of animals. This zoo emphasises the emotional connection and is a great way to spend a Wednesday afternoon. The food options are over-prices, so bring your own snacks if you want them.

Watch free perfor-mances

Manhattan

SummerStage takes place from June through early September, and features over 100 free performances at 17 parks. Shakespeare in the Park, held also in Central Park. Top actors like Meryl Streep and Al Pacino have taken the stage in years past! Prospect Park has its own open-air summer concert and events series. Celebrate Brooklyn.

Go to a Free outdoor cinema

In summertime you can see free films at the River to River Festival (www.rivertorivernyc.com; at Hudson River Park in Manhattan and at Brooklyn Bridge Park www.brooklyn-bridgepark.org

Chck out the free HBO Bryant Park Summer Film Festival (www.bryantpark.org; hmid-Jun–Aug) screenings on Monday nights.

Hear Gospel Music
Many churches, especially in Harlem and Brooklyn, open up their doors on Wednesdays and Sundays for religious services with incredible gospel music.

Watch Free Live music

BAMcafe in Brooklyn has free concerts (world music, R&B, jazz, rock) on select Friday and Saturday nights. In Harlem, Marjorie Eliot opens her home for free jazz jams on Sunday. If you like jazz, visit Blue Note, Birdland or Village Vanguard. The atmosphere is electrifying during the live sets. Look at https://www.bam.org/programs/bamcafe-live to see when they have no cover charge days.

Explore the markets

Markets are a fun and eye-opening plunge into local culture and, unless you succumb to the persistent vendors, it will cost you nothing. Don't expect to find the bargain of a lifetime but Chinatown is always great browsing plus there are cheap dumplings, pork buns and hand-pulled noodles! Brooklyn Flea. LIC Flea Market, Queens Night Market, Union Square Greenmarket. Chelsea Market, Red Hook Food Vendors (go if you love Latin American food) are all worth checking out.

Stiles Farmers Market is a Neighbourhood grocer offering a wide variety of fresh produce & baked goods at discount prices.

Century 21, have designer goods for cheap - gets very crowded on Saturdays and Sundays.

La Marqueta (aka Park Avenue Retail Market) is the oldest public market in New York City. It opened in 1936. The public markets were meant to create indoor space to replace open-air pushcart markets, and Park Ave in East Harlem was the epicenter but merely became an extension of them.

INSIDER MONEY SAVING TIP

You can find sample sales by looking for flyers and sidewalk billboard in the Garment District (34th - 40th Streets, between 5th and 9th Avenue). Many sample sales discount designer goods from 70% to even 90% off.

Go to an auction

Founded in 1766, Christie's is a famous British auction house. Christie's New York is always free to visit. They have guest lectures, a beautiful gallery with diverse exhibits all for FREE!
Address: Rockefeller Center

Watch Free comedy

New York City has always cast a melodramatic profile. There are over 230 free comedy shows a month throughout NYC, Brooklyn, and Queens! Here are the best of the crop:

• The Lantern Comedy Club
• "Hot Soup" at Irish Exit. Midtown East. Tuesdays at 8pm.
• "Gandhi, Is That You" at Lucky Jack's. LES. Wednesdays at 9pm.
• "Whiplash" at Upright Citizens Brigade. Chelsea. Mondays at 11pm.
• "Broken Comedy" at Bar Matchless. Greenpoint.
• Open mic night at Legion Bar. Williamsburg.

For the latest show times visit freestandupnyc.com

INSIDER CULTURAL INSIGHT

New Yorkers love to talk, but don't ask someone you don't know what they pay in rent or what they are paid in salary. It's considered offensive.

Chill out in Central Park

After many years of debate over the location, the park's construction finally began in 1857, based on the winner of a park design contest, the "Greensward Plan," Affectionately known as 'The Lungs of New York', Central Park is one of the most beautiful parts of New York and you can see why locals love it so much.

Stretching from 59th St in Midtown Manhattan to 110th St in Harlem its a refuge from the cities chaos. It has free wifi, so you can still stay on, if you want to.

INSIDER MONEY SAVING TIP

If central Park is overcrowded head to Governors Island its home to a 25-foot hill that offers a 360-degree view of the city's harbour.

INSIDER MONEY SAVING TIP

Sara Roosevelt Park – bordered by Canal, Chrystie, Houston, and Forsyth streets – is a hidden sanctuary for kids with basketball, volleyball, and handball courts, soccer fields, five playgrounds, and a community garden.

Pumphouse Park

If you visit in spring or summer then floral Pumphouse Park is a must-see. But even in the colder months the park along the Hudson River will be filled with families playing in the snow.

Go Church Hopping

Not only exceptional architecturally and historically, New York's churches contain exquisite art, artefacts and other priceless treasures. Best of all, entry to general areas within them is, in most cases, free. Do respect the fact that although many of the places of worship are also major tourist attractions. Trinity Church Wall Street, St. Patrick's Cathedral (already mentioned) Grace Church, Hillsong Church Manhattan, The Brooklyn Tabernacle are the best of the crop.

Thrift shop

Thrift stores in NYC are some of the best in the world, but theres stiff competition for the best bargains. Go early and bring snacks for energy to hunt down designer pieces. Here are the best thrift stores: Lot Less Closeouts. 206 W 40th St, Artists and Fleas at Chelsea Market. 88 Tenth Ave, 15th Street (btwn W 15th & 16th St), Chelsea. Philip Williams Posters. 122 Chambers St and Housing Works Thrift Shop. What you want to look for are the ones located in affluent areas with low-income foot-fall. If you're not familiar with the area and asking around hasn't returned any results, here's what you can do. Google for the most expensive area to live in NYC, sometimes they are a little outside the city. Then put the American term Thrift store into Google Maps. Start with the most expensive and work your way through until the middle-tier ones. You will be surprised what you find.

Hunt for rare first editions

Pay a visit to Westsider Rare & used Books store offering fiction, art books, children's literature & rock music albums. You never know what you will uncover.

Go Book Shopping

Bookoff offers a huge range of paperback books for low prices.

Address: 49 W 45th Street.

Explore NYC Street art

Much of what can now be defined as modern street art has well-documented origins dating from New York City's graffiti boom, with its infancy in the 1960s, maturation in the 1970s, and peaking with the spray-painted fullcar subway train murals of the 1980s centered in the Bronx.

Here are the best places to spot the most incredible urban canvasses today:

- Welling Court Mural Project, Astoria.
- First Street Green Art Park, East Village.
- The Bowery Wall, Nolita.
- Freeman Alley, Lower East Side.
- The Bushwick Collective, Bushwick.
- Graffiti Hall of Fame, East Harlem.
- Tuff City, Bronx.

- Coney Art Walls, Coney Island.

Galleries

- Centre-fuge **Public Art** Project's rotating gallery.
- Lower East Side's Freeman Alley.
- Graffiti Hall of Fame's Latin American art.
- 'Love Vandal' by Nick Walker's
- Welling Court Mural Project, Queens' premier street-art
- gallery.

Escape the crowds

The title sounds like an oxymoron in New York, which boasts 67 million visitors in 2019 but despite this huge concentration of people you can find quiet spots. If you are easily overwhelmed by crowds visit the obvious attractions as early as possible, peak people flow is 11 am to 5 pm so get up early to enjoy the attractions serenely. Luckily New York also has some hidden gems that aren't commercialised or too crowded most of the time. Here are the best:

• The Morgan Library and Museum. This library belonged to fa-ther of JP Morgan. You can visit for free on Fridays between 7pm and 9pm. The interior is stunning and absolutely worth the trip.
• Jamaica Bay Wildlife Refuge in Queens is an unbelievable quiiet wildlife reserve you can take the metro to.
• There are three community Gardens, one at 6th and Avenue B, Creative Little Garden and La Plaza Cultural which are free and peaceful.
• Greenacre Park - One of the best ways to escape the hustle and bustle of Manhattan is to visit the waterfall at Greenacre Park. This private, but publicly accessible park, located between 2nd and 3rd Avenue, spans 6,360 square feet and features a 25-foot waterfall.

Get something totally for free

You could furnish an entire apartment pretty decently with all the things people are giving away in New York.

If you find you need to buy something, whether that be a charger or torch in New York check free stuff in New York sites before you buy. You can often find incredible freebies here that will cost you only the time to pick them up. Here is the best free stuff group in New York: https://www.facebook.com/groups/freestuffinnyc/

Not super cheap but loved

SUMMIT One Vanderbilt

'The Summit Ascent ticket prices range from $53-$69. This ticket type provides general admission to the Summit One Vanderbilt observatory as well as a thrilling glass elevator journey in the Ascent elevator that travels over 1,200 feet in the airThe best time to visit the Summit One Vanderbilt is early morning or one hour before sunset. Early morning you'll bump into the least crowds and one hour before sunset, you can catch the best views and capture great photos.'

The Empire State Building and Top of the Rock are included for free on all tourist passes so if observation decks are high on your list of must-sees, buying a tourist pass is a cheaper way to visit them.

NYC Food and Drink hacks

Eat dinner during happy hour

New York restaurants are pricey, look for happy hours, they can be a great way to save money - 4:00pm and goes until 8:00pm (or closing). Food specials can include pre-fix menus, 50% off starters, $1 oysters or 20% off the food menu depending on the restaurant.

Enjoy Best bang for your buck all-you-can-eat

A B Sushi Japanese is an all you can eat buffet that will blow your mind. I cannot believe a place like this exists in New York.

Delicious sushi is a given in NYC, however delicious sushi and being reasonably priced is a rare occurrence. Go for lunch and pay $18 for all you can eat sushi. All you can eat buffets are a great way to stock on on nutritious food while travelling. Dishes like fish are normally expensive, but here you can chow down on your omega 3's for much less. Don't drink much water or eat tons of rice and you'll get more than your money's worth.

Enjoy an Amazing falafel sandwich for $5

Oasis in Williamsburg (right outside the Bedford avenue stop) do amazing falafel sandwich for $5 or chicken kebab for $6. Also the green taco truck on Bedford Avenue (parked outside the Starbucks) has the best burrito I've had in New York for $8 (get the steak one).

Taste the Best bagel in town

The best bagel in the city comes from Ess-A-Bagel in midtown east. $5 but absolutely amazing. The bagels come with huge amounts of fillings and eating one will be one of your favourite New York moments.

Address: W 36th Street

Find deals to eat out

Great sites to visit include Yelp Deals, Groupon, LivingSocial, and Valpak. You can also find coupons at places such as your local hotel, bus or train stations, and the airport, so keep your eyes open.

Free coffee refill

Save a little cash while *still* feeding your caffeine habit, you can get free refills at Thrillist an ever growing New York City coffee chain, which serves Seattle's Caffe refills on iced coffee and filter coffees.

Free Food

And if you're really hard up you can go to The New York City ISKCON Temple for free food For ethical reasons I would only go here, if you're really struggling, and if you are, firstly, I'm sorry, that sucks. Make sure to check out our section on finding work while travelling. Things like teaching English online are easy to get started.

Must-try New York Street Foods

New York has so many good restaurants. But there are also dishes that are best enjoyed on the streets. Here are the ones you must-try:

Pastrami sandwiches - New York's Sussman Volk is generally credited with producing the first pastrami sandwich in the United States in 1887. Volk, a kosher butcher and New York immigrant from Lithuania, claimed he got the recipe from a Romanian friend in exchange for storing the friend's luggage while the friend returned to Romania.
Baked pretzels.

New York cheesecake - The cheesecake wasn't invented in New York. But the city's immigrant bakers tweaked and touted a version that became famous around the world. For centuries, people baked cheesecakes across Europe using a savory farmers' cheese, said Joan Nathan, an expert on Jewish-American cooking.

Bagels - It is believed that bagels made their way to New

York with the migration of Eastern European Jewish immi grants in the late 1800s. By 1900, 70 bakeries existed on the Lower East Side, and in 1907, the International Beigel Bakers' Union was created to monopolize the production bagel production in the city.Sep 6, 2017

Pizza - New York-style pizza began with the opening of America's first pizzeria, Lombardi's, by Gennaro Lombardi in the Little Italy neighborhood of Manhattan in 1905, which served large, wide pies. An employee, Antonio Totonno Pero, cooked the pizzas and slices were sold for 5¢

Falafel
Taco's and Burritos. You will find at least five of these being sold from a street food vendor on every corner.

Cheap Eats

If you tire of eating street foods go to these sit-down restaurants in New York to fill your stomach without emptying your wallet.. Here are the Best Cheap Eats in NYC for Under $5!

Joe's Pizza is a Greenwich Village institution where you can grab pizza under $3!

Toasties
Address: 148 W 49th St A
Quick tasty sandwiches under $5 close to Times Square.

Patzeria Perfect Pizza
Address: 231 W 46th St
Cheap and delicious pizza also Near Times Square.

Kopitiam
Address: 51 E Broadway
Cheap delicious Malaysian.

Tiki Chick
Fried Chicken Sandwiches under 5 on the Upper West sider.

2Bro's Pizza
Offer 2 slices and a soda for $3 in the East Village.

Two Hands Corn Dogs near the New Museum offers Potato Corn Dogs for $4.

Mikey Likes it, also in the East Village has waffle ice cream sandwiches for under $5.

All of these local restaurants have mains under $8.

Note: Download the offline map on Google maps, (instructions 1. go to app 2. select offline apps in the left sidebar 3. go to the area you want to download 4. click download). Then simply type the restaurant names in to navigate, add it to your favourites by clicking the star icon so you can see where the cheap eats are when you're out and about to avoid wasting your money at hyped tourist joints)

Los Tacos
A restaurant with over 20 outlets in NYC. Bustling taqueria serving tacos, quesadillas & aguas frescas in a street-style set-up (no seating).

Vanessa's Dumpling House
Steamed-while-you-wait dumplings & other Chinese fare served in basic surrounds.

88 Lan Zhou Handmade Noodles
Bare-bones Chinese noodle joint slinging classic, house-made-dough dishes (no alcohol & cash only).

Cheeky Sandwiches
A hip sandwich shop offering a select menu of po' boys & other Big Easy bites in a tiny storefront.

Taqueria Diana
This small, utilitarian Mexican restaurant serves tacos, burritos, nachos, roast chicken & more.

Baohaus
Savory Taiwanese steamed buns are the specialty of this bare-bones East Village eatery.

Margon
Small Latin counter-service spot serving Cuban sandwiches, American breakfasts & salads.

goa taco
Cozy counter-service joint offering creative, globally-inspired tacos in paratha shells.

Manousheh

Brick-walled eatery specializing in savory & sweet Lebanese flatbreads baked in-house.

Blue Collar

Counter-serve burger joint serving griddled burgers, fries & handmade shakes in a retro space.

Thelewala

Bustling spot that's open late turning out classic Indian street eats in a compact, mod storefront.

Papaya King

Counter-service eatery serving budget-friendly hot dogs & papaya drinks in a no-frills setting.

Sons of Thunder

Customizable poké bowls plus burgers & shakes in counter-serve digs with a big, airy seating area.

ilili Box

Inventive Lebanese bites are served at this food-stand off-shoot of a local, upscale restaurant.

Egg Shop

Sunny little cafe focusing on everything egg including creative sandwiches, fancy Benedicts & more.

Mimi Cheng's Dumplings

Several different Chinese dumplings made from family recipes star at this tiny spot with few seats.

Mamoun's Falafel

Longtime local Middle Eastern chain serving falafel, shawarma, kebabs & more in a traditional space.
The falafels are always filling , cheap and the white sauce will dance on your tongue.

Little Saigon Pearl

Good food and cheap! Definitely my favorite Vietnamese in New York.

Won Dee Siam

One of the best and cheapest Thai restaurants in Manhattan (on 9th Avenue and 52nd Street). Ask for the "special menu" they only give to their Thai regulars. It won't disappoint.

Misirizzi

4th b/w Bowery & Lafayette

Get the squid ink pasta.

Boulud Sud

The pre-theater prix-fixe meal is a bargain. A celebrity chef cooks you a three course fixed price meal for $65 a person.

Schmackary's

If you like cookies, Schmackary's is a must visit spot.

The frying pan

It's an old boat turned into a bar/ restaurant. Happy hour is 5pm - 7pm and unmissable. The boat is open May to October.

Nightlife – Bars & Clubs

If you don't go out in New York you'll miss out on some great venues – the clubs and bars make it hard to catch some sleep ibut prices for indulging nocturnal desires aren't cheap. Here are some places to drink on the cheap - all with beers under $4!

- Johnny's Bar
- Rudy's Bar & Grill
- Local 138
- Jimmy's Corner
- Barcelona bar in Hell's Kitchen - Kind of a dive but so en-tertain-ing & they have very cheap drinks for Manhattan.
- Botanica Bar The place is a bit on the dark side, but the prices and happy hour make braving it worth-while.

INSIDER TIP

PDT (Please Don't Tell) is a tiny speakeasy concealed behind a hot-dog joint. You need reservations to visit this secret bar. If it's your first time, try to avoid booking your reservation when the bar opens so that you can experience the entrance on your own. You enter through the phone booth.

INSIDER HISTORICAL INSIGHT

If you're into history pay a visit to Fraunces Tavern on Pearl Street. You can Study a lock of George Washington's hair — and his tooth — at Fraunces Tavern. A renovated historic tavern with a George Washington link offering pub eats & live music on weekends.

Don't leave New York without seeing these attractions (if only from outside)

Statue of Liberty
Iconic National Monument opened in 1886, offering guided tours, a museum & city views.

Times Square
Bustling destination in the heart of the Theater District known for bright lights, shopping & shows.

Metropolitan Museum of Art
A grand setting for one of the world's greatest collections of art, from ancient to contemporary.

Brooklyn Bridge
Beloved, circa-1883 landmark connecting Manhattan & Brooklyn via a unique stone-&-steel design.

Rockefeller Center
Famous complex that's home to TV studios, plus a seasonal ice rink & giant Christmas tree.

Grand Central Terminal
Iconic train station known for its grand facade & main concourse, also offering shops & dining.

The Battery
Historic park with Ellis Island & Statue of Liberty views & ferry service to both islands.

Theatre District
 The Theater District is the teeming heart of Midtown West. In the pedestrian plazas of Times Square, costumed characters beckon to energetic crowds.

Liberty Island
Audio & guided tours are offered on this iconic island featuring the Statue of Liberty & a museum.

9/11 Memorial
Plaza, pools & exhibits honoring victims of 1993 & 2001 WTC terrorist attacks. Free timed admission. A visit to the 9/11 Memorial is an emotional experience for many. Many New Yorkers lost family members or were permanently traumatized by the attacks.

SoHo, Manhattan
Designer boutiques, fancy chain stores and high-end art galleries make trendy SoHo a top shopping destination, especially for out-of-towners. Known for its elegant cast-iron-facades and cobblestones.

Coney Island
Coney Island morphs into an entertainment destination each summer with its theme park.

American Museum of Natural History
From dinosaurs to outer space and everything in between, this huge museum showcases natural wonders.

Solomon R. Guggenheim Museum
Frank Lloyd Wright–designed modern-art museum with an architecturally significant spiral rotunda.

The Plaza
Iconic 19th-century lodging offering fine dining & afternoon tea, plus a champagne bar & a spa.

Greenwich Village
The epicenter of the city's 1960s counterculture movement, the tree-lined streets of Greenwich Village are now a hub of Jazz clubs and Off-Broadway Theaters.

Bryant Park
Green space behind the NY Public Library's main branch, with 4 acres, a cafe and other food kiosks.

Flatiron Building
Architect Daniel Burnham's iconic 1902 triangular tower nicknamed for its clothes iron look.

DUMBO
Trendy Dumbo's cobblestone streets and converted Brooklyn warehouse buildings are the backdrop for independent boutiques, high-end restaurants and trendy cafes.

Little Italy
Little Italy welcomes a heavily tourist crowd to its high concentration of souvenir shops and traditional Italian eateries and bakeries.

Union Square
The lively Union Square neighborhood is anchored by it's namesake pedestrian plaza and bustling park, which attracts a mix of professionals, street artists, students and protesters.

Lower East Side
The eclectic Lower East Side is where gritty alleys and tenement-style buildings mix with upscale apartments and chic boutiques. Nighttime draws hip, young crowds.

Washington Square Park
Historic Greenwich Village concrete-&-green park known for its stately arch & prime people-watching.

Financial District
This is the city's buzzing financial heart, home to Wall Street and glittering skyscrapers. Sidewalks bustle during the week and, after work, young professionals fill the restaurants and bars.

Intrepid Sea, Air & Space Museum
Flight museum on an aircraft carrier whose exhibits include a Concorde, submarine & space shuttle.

Meatpacking District
The Meatpacking District is a hip commercial area on the far west side. It's home to the Whitney Museum of American Art and high-end designer clothing stores.

Manhattan Bridge
Opened in 1909, this suspension bridge between Brooklyn & Manhattan.

Is the tap water drink-able?

Yes.

How much can you save haggling here?

Gentle haggling is common at markets in NYC. Haggling in stores is generally unacceptable, although some good-humoured bargaining at smaller artisan or craft shops is cool if you are making multiple purchases.

Enjoy your first Day for under $20

Start early by visiting the American Museum of Natural History for free. Then great a cheap bagel and coffee and take a couple of hours to explore Central Park. Enjoy highlights such as Strawberry Fields, Sheeps Meadow, the Bow Bridge and the Bethesda Fountain. Follow the aromas to one of the numerous delis on 7th Ave. Explore Midtown Manhattan, visiting Times Square, Fifth Avenue, the Madison Square Garden and much more. Take the 1 train from Times Square to South Ferry. Jump on board the Staten Island ferry for unforgettable views of the Statue of Liberty. Take the 1 train back up to Christopher St/Sheridan Square. Get take away pizza in 'Bleecker St Pizza' both in the West Village. Wander down Bleecker Street until you come to MacDougal St - the heart of Greenwich Village. Go for a beer in one of the many bars before heading home to sleep.

What you need to Need to Know before you go

Currency: Dollar
Language: English
Money: Widely available ATMs.
Visas: The US Visa Waiver Program allows nationals of 38 countries to enter the US without a visa, but
you must fill out an ESTA application before departing.
http://www.doyouneedvisa.com/
Time: GMT - 5
When to Go
High Season: July and August.
Shoulder: May, April, June
Low Season: September to May.
Important Numbers
113 Ambulance
112 Police

Getting out of New York cheaply

Bus
Megabus
Booking ahead can save you up to 98% of the cost of the ticket. Check for destinations from NYC.

Plane
At the time of writing Spirit are offering the cheapest flights onwards. Take advantage of discounts and specials. Sign up for e-newsletters from local carriers including Spirit to learn about special fares. Be careful with cheap airlines, most will allow hand-luggage only, and some charge for anything that is not a backpack. Check their websites before booking if you need to take luggage.

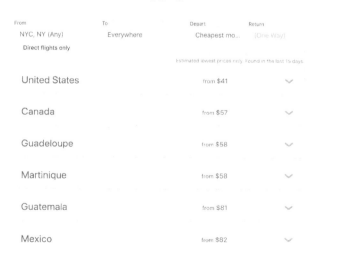

From	To	Depart	Return
NYC, NY (Any)	Everywhere	Cheapest mo...	(One Way)
Direct flights only			
		Estimated lowest prices only. Found in the last 15 days	
United States		from $41	∨
Canada		from $57	∨
Guadeloupe		from $58	∨
Martinique		from $58	∨
Guatemala		from $81	∨
Mexico		from $82	∨

Airport Lounges

You don't need to be flying business or first class to enjoy an airport lounge. Here are three methods you can use to access lounges at New York airports:

- Get or use a credit card that gives free lounge access. NerdWallet has a good write-up about cards that offer free lounge access. www.nerdwallet.com/best/credit-cards/airport-lounge-access

- Buy onetime access. They start at $23 and often include free showers and free drinks and food.

- Find free access with the LoungeBuddy app. You pay an annual fee of $25 to use the app. Iwww.loungebuddy.com/

Avoid these tourist traps or scams

Scams and trickery are the scourge of a traveler's budget and unfortunately scams abound in NYC, and particularly near the attractions. If someone approaches you and you fear their intentions just say 'sorry, no english.' and walk on. A well known scam is scammers selling fake tickets to get onto Liberty island, the island holding the Statue of Liberty. Only one company, Statue Cruises, sells these tickets, buy them online to avoid being conned by official looking sales-men - there are tons of conman there and they look legit. It's not a scam but don't get on the local subway trains, they will take twice the time. Also don't stop in the middle of the sidewalk to take pictures - locals will shout at you.

 pickpocketing isn't a popular crime in NYC like it is in some cities. Grab and run is more common.

RECAP: Enjoy a $5,000 trip to New York for $350

Stay in East Williamsburg

This is the best neighbourhood for people who want to stay outside of Manhattan and experience Brooklyn. We felt totally safe the whole time. The area around is great- very nice shops and bars. Most importantly its close to the L line so you can get anywhere. It is the area with the best bang for your buck, and if you don't want to stay in hostels you can find an Airbnb room for $30 a night here. Potential saving $600.

Blind book hotels and or use pricelines express deals

The cheapest hotel deals are available when you 'blind book'. You don't know the name of the hotel before you book. Use Last Minute Top Secret hotels or pricelines express deals and you can find a four star hotel from $60 a night in New York!

Use too good to go

Pick up 'magic bags' for dinner to save an absolute fortune on restaurant food. Just remember to pack a spork (a fork, knife and spoon) if you're staying at a hotel.

Restaurant deals

A lot of restaurants in NYC offer a midday menu for lunch at around $12 or happy hour deals, If you're on a budget, but like eating out, consider doing your dining in the daytime or during happy hours. Potential saving $150.

Dine in cheap Michelin star restaurants
You can enjoy $500 menu's from $30 in NYC. It would practically be criminal not to try some of New York's amazing Michelin star restaurants. Potential saving: $2,000

Have a picnic
Make like a local, go to Sheep's Meadow in Central Park when the sun is shining with some pizza and beers.

Go to museums/ attractions on their free days
Get cultured for free, or for cheap, by knowing the gallery and museum free days. The average traveller spends $250 on attractions in NYC, but there's an abundance of free or cheap attractions if you time your visit right. Potential saving $250.

Get broadway tickets super cheap
Use any of the methods we outlined to score $400 tickets for $50 or less. Potential saving $350.

Get incredible views from the Roosevelt tram and ferries
If you want to see New York in all its glory at night take the Roosevelt tram. Just $6 return.

Get out cheaply
If you're travelling around the states you can get super cheap onward journeys starting from $5 with megabus.com

Money Mistakes in New York

Cost	Impact	Solution	Note
Using your home currency	Some credit card rates charge for every transaction in another currency. Check carefully before you use it	Use a prepaid currency card like Wise Multi-Currency Debit Card.	If you wouldn't borrow money from a friend or relative for your trip, don't borrow it from a credit card company.
Not using the subway	$33 for unlimited travel will enable you to go all over the city for an entire week. Taxi's would cost you hundreds and result in a lot of time lost to traffic.	Buy a Subway pass	
Buying bottled water	At $1 a bottle, this is a cost that can mount up quickly	Refill from the tap. Bring an on the go water filter bottle like Water-to-go or use life-straw.	
Eating like a tourist	Eating at tourist traps can triple your bill. Choose wisely	Star cheap eats on google maps so you're never far from one	
Not visiting attractions during their free times	You can save $500 on entrance fees just going during the free times	Make an itinerary.	

The secret to saving HUGE amounts of money when travelling to New York is...

Your mindset. Money is an emotional topic, if you associate words like cheapskate, Miser (and its £9.50 to go into Charles Dickens New York house, oh the Irony) with being thrifty when traveling you are likely to say 'F-it' and spend your money needlessly because you associate pain with saving money. You pay now for an immediate reward. Our brains are prehistoric; they focus on surviving day to day. Travel companies and hotels know this and put trillions into making you believe you will be happier when you spend on their products or services. Our poor brains are up against outdated programming and an onslaught of advertisements bombarding us with the message: spending money on travel equals PLEASURE. To correct this carefully lodged propaganda in your frontal cortex, you need to imagine your future self.

Saving money does not make you a cheapskate. It makes you smart. How do people get rich? They invest their money. They don't go out and earn it; they let their money earn more money. So every time you want to spend money, imagine this: while you travel, your money is working for you, not you for money. While you sleep, the money, you've invested is going up and up. That's a pleasure a pricey entrance fee can't give you. Thinking about putting your money to work for you tricks your brain into believing you are not withholding pleasure from yourself, you are saving your money to invest so you can go to even more amazing places. You are thus turning thrifty travel into a pleasure fueled sport.

When you've got money invested - If you want to splash your cash on a first-class airplane seat - you can. I can't tell you how to invest your money, only that you should. Saving $20 on taxis doesn't seem like much, but over time you could save upwards of $15,000 a year, which is a deposit for a house which you can rent on Airbnb to finance more travel. Your brain making money looks like your brain on cocaine, so tell yourself saving money is making money.

Scientists have proved that imagining your future self is the easiest way to associate pleasure with saving money. You can download FaceApp — which will give you a picture of what you will look like older and grayer, or you can take a deep breath just before spending money and ask yourself if you will regret the purchase later.

The easiest ways to waste money traveling are:

Getting a taxi. The solution to this is to always download the google map before you go. Many taxi drivers will drive you around for 15 minutes when the place you were trying to get to is a 5-minute walk… remember while not getting an overpriced taxi to tell yourself, 'I am saving money to free myself for more travel.' Spending money on overpriced food when hungry. The solution: carry snacks. A banana and an apple will cost you, in most places, less than a dollar.

Spending on entrance fees to top-rated attractions. If you really want to do it, spend the money happily. If you're conflicted, sleep on it. I don't regret spending $200 on a sky dive over the Great Barrier Reef; I regret going to the top of the shard on a cloudy day in London for $60. Only you can know, but make sure it's your decision and not the marketing directors at said top-rated attraction.

Telling yourself 'you only have the chance to see/eat/experience it now'. While this might be true, make sure YOU WANT to spend the money. Money spent is money you can't invest, and often you can have the same experience for much less.

You can experience luxurious travel on a small budget, which will trick your brain into thinking you're already a high-roller, which will mean you'll be more likely to act like one and invest your money. Stay in five-star hotels for $5 by booking on the day of your stay on booking.com to enjoy last-minute deals. You can go to fancy restaurants using daily deal sites. Ask your airline about last-minute upgrades to first-class or business. I paid $100 extra on a $179 ticket to Cuba from Germany to be bumped to Business Class. When you ask, it will surprise you what you can get both at hotels and airlines.

Travel, as the saying goes, is the only thing you spend money on that makes you richer. You can easily waste money, making it difficult to enjoy that metaphysical wealth. The biggest money saving secret is to turn bargain hunting into a pleasurable activity, not an annoyance. Budgeting consciously can be fun, don't feel disappointed because you don't spend the $60 to go into an attraction. Feel good because soon that $60 will soon earn money for you. Meaning, you'll have the time and money to enjoy more metaphysical wealth while your bank balance increases.

So there it is. You can save a small fortune by being strategic with your trip planning. We've arranged everything in the guide to offer the best bang for your buck. Which means we took the view that if it's not an excellent investment for your money, we wouldn't include it. Why would a guide called 'Super Cheap' include lots of overpriced attractions? That said, if you think we've missed something or have unanswered questions, ping me an email: philgtang@gmail.com I'm on central Europe time and usually reply within 8 hours of getting your mail. We like to think of our guide books as evolving organisms helping our readers travel better cheaper. We use reader questions via email to update this book year round so you'll be helping other readers and yourself.

Don't put your dreams off!

Time is a currency you never get back and travel is its greatest return on investment. Plus, now you know you can visit New York for a fraction of the price most would have you believe.

View from Brooklyn Bridge

Thank you for reading

Dear **Lovely Reader**,

If you have found this book useful, please consider writing a quick review on Amazon.

One person from every 1000 readers leaves a review on Amazon. It would mean more than you could ever know if you were one of our 1 in 1000 people to take the time to write a brief review.

Thank you so much for reading again and for spending your time and investing your trips future in Super Cheap Insider Guides. One last note, please don't listen to anyone who says 'Oh no, you can't visit New York on a budget'. Unlike you, they didn't have this book. You can do ANYWHERE on a budget with the right insider advice and planning. Sure, learning to travel to New York on a budget that doesn't compromise on anything or drastically compromise on safety or comfort levels is a skill, but this guide has done the detective work for you. Now it is time for you to put the advice into action.

Phil and the Super Cheap Insider Guides Team

P.S If you need any more super cheap tips we'd love to hear from you e-mail me at philgtang@gmail.com, we have a lot of contacts in every region, so if there's a specific bargain you're hunting we can help you find it.

DISCOVER YOUR NEXT VACATION

✅ **LUXURY ON A BUDGET APPROACH**

✅ **CHOOSE FROM 107 DESTINATIONS**

✅ **EACH BOOK PACKED WITH REAL-TIME LOCAL TIPS**

All are available in Paperback and e-book on Amazon: https://www.amazon.com/dp/B09C2DHQG5

Several are available as audiobooks. You can watch excerpts of ALL for FREE on YouTube: https://youtube.com/channel/UCxo9YV8-M9P1cFosU-Gjnqg

Super Cheap ADELAIDE 2023
Super Cheap ALASKA 2023
Super Cheap AMSTERDAM 2023
Super Cheap ANTIGUA 2023
Super Cheap ANTARCTICA 2023
Super Cheap AUSTIN 2023
Super Cheap BANGKOK 2023
Super Cheap BARBADOS 2023
Super Cheap BARCELONA 2023
Super Cheap BATH 2023
Super Cheap BELFAST 2023
Super Cheap BERMUDA 2023
Super Cheap BERLIN 2023
Super Cheap BIRMINGHAM 2023
Super Cheap BORA BORA 2023
Super Cheap BORDEAUX 2023
Super Cheap BRUGES 2023
Super Cheap BUDAPEST 2023
Super Cheap Bahamas 2023
Super Cheap Great Barrier Reef 2023

Super Cheap CABO 2023
Super Cheap CALGARY 2023
Super Cheap CAMBRIDGE 2023
Super Cheap CANCUN 2023
Super Cheap CAPPADOCIA 2023
Super Cheap CAPRI 2023
Super Cheap CARCASSONNE 2023
Super Cheap CHAMPAGNE REGION 2023
Super Cheap CHIANG MAI 2023
Super Cheap CHICAGO 2023
Super Cheap COPENHAGEN 2023
Super Cheap DOHA 2023
Super Cheap DOMINICAN REPUBLIC 2023
Super Cheap DUBAI 2023
Super Cheap DUBLIN 2023
Super Cheap EDINBURGH 2023
Super Cheap FLORENCE 2023
Super Cheap GALAPAGOS ISLANDS 2023
Super Cheap GALWAY 2023
Super Cheap HAVANA 2023
Super Cheap HELSINKI 2023
Super Cheap HONG KONG 2023
Super Cheap HONOLULU 2023
Super Cheap INNSBRUCK 2023
Super Cheap ISTANBUL 2023
Super Cheap KUALA LUMPUR 2023
Super Cheap LA 2023
Super Cheap LAPLAND 2023
Super Cheap LAS VEGAS 2023
Super Cheap LIMA 2023
Super Cheap LISBON 2023
Super Cheap LIVERPOOL 2023
Super Cheap LONDON 2023
Super Cheap MACHU PICHU 2023
Super Cheap MALAGA 2023

Super Cheap MALDIVES 2023
Super Cheap Machu Pichu 2023
Super Cheap MELBOURNE 2023
Super Cheap MIAMI 2023
Super Cheap MONACO 2023
Super Cheap Milan 2023
Super Cheap Munich 2023
Super Cheap NASHVILLE 2023
Super Cheap NEW ORLEANS 2023
Super Cheap NEW YORK 2023
Super Cheap NORWAY 2023
Super Cheap PARIS 2023
Super Cheap PRAGUE 2023
Super Cheap SAN FRANCISCO 2023
Super Cheap Santorini 2023
Super Cheap SEYCHELLES 2023
Super Cheap SINGAPORE 2023
Super Cheap SYDNEY 2023
Super Cheap ST LUCIA 2023
Super Cheap TORONTO 2023
Super Cheap TURKS AND CAICOS 2023
Super Cheap TURIN 2023
Super Cheap VENICE 2023
Super Cheap VIENNA 2023
Super Cheap WASHINGTON 2023
Super Cheap YORK 2023
Super Cheap YOSEMITE 2023
Super Cheap ZURICH 2023
Super Cheap ZANZIBAR 2023

Bonus Travel Hacks

I've included these bonus travel hacks to help you plan and enjoy your trip to New York cheaply, joyfully, and smoothly. Perhaps they will even inspire you to start or renew a passion for long-term travel.

Common pitfalls when it comes to allocating money to <u>your desires</u> while traveling

Beware of Malleable mental accounting

Let's say you budgeted spending only $30 per day in New York but then you say well if I was at home I'd be spending $30 on food as an everyday purchase so you add another $30 to your budget. Don't fall into that trap as the likelihood is you still have expenses at home even if its just the cost of keeping your freezer going.

Beware of impulse purchases in New York

Restaurants that you haven't researched and just idle into can sometimes turn out to be great, but more often, they turn out to suck, especially if they are near tourist attractions. Make yourself a travel itinerary including where you'll eat breakfast and lunch. Dinner is always more expensive, so the meal best to enjoy at home or as a takeaway. This book is full of incredible cheap eats. All you have to do is plan to go to them.

Social media and FOMO (Fear of Missing Out)

'The pull of seeing acquaintances spend money on travel can often be a more powerful motivator to spend more while traveling than seeing an advertisement.' Beware of what you allow to influence you and go back to the question, what's the best money I can spend today?

Now-or-never sales strategies

One reason tourists are targeted by salespeople is the success of the now-or-never strategy. If you don't spend the money now… your never get the opportunity again. Rarely is this true.

Instead of spending your money on something you might not actually desire, take five minutes. Ask yourself, do I really want this? And return to the answer in five minutes. Your body will either say an absolute yes with a warm, excited feeling or a no with a weak, obscure feeling.

Unexpected costs

"Holding on to anger is like grasping a hot coal with the intent of throwing it at someone else; you only hurt yourself." The Buddha.

One downside to traveling is unexpected costs. When these spring up from airlines, accommodation providers, tours and on and on, they feel like a punch in the gut. During the pandemic my earnings fell to 20% of what they are normally. No one was traveling, no one was buying travel guides. My accountant out of nowhere significantly raised his fee for the year despite the fact there was a lot less money to count. I was so angry I consulted a lawyer who told me you will spend more taking him to court than you will paying his bill. I had to get myself into a good feeling place before I paid his bill, so I googled how to feel good paying someone who has scammed you.

The answer: Write down that you will receive 10 times the amount you are paying from an unexpected source. I did that. Four months later, the accountant wrote to me. He had

applied for a COVID subsidy for me and I would receive…
you guessed it almost exactly 10 times his fee.

Make of that what you want. I don't wish to get embroiled in
a conversation about what many term 'woo-woo', but the
result of my writing that I would receive 10 times the
amount made me feel much, much better when paying him.
And ultimately, that was a gift in itself. So next time some
airline or train operator or hotel/ Airbnb sticks you with an
unexpected fee, immediately write that you will receive 10
times the amount you are paying from an unexpected
source. Rise your vibe and skip the added price of feeling
angry.

Hack your allocations for your New York Trip

"The best trick for saving is to eliminate the decision to save." Perry Wright of Duke University.

Put the money you plan to spend in New York on a pre-paid card in the local currency. This cuts out two problems - not knowing how much you've spent and totally avoiding expensive currency conversion fees.

You could even create separate spaces. This much for transportation, this for tours/entertainment, accommodation and food. We are reluctant to spend money that is pre-assigned to categories or uses.

Write that you want to enjoy a $3,000 trip for $500 to your New York trip. Countless research shows when you put goals in writing, you have a higher chance of following through.

Spend all the money you want to on buying experiences in New York

"Experiences are like good relatives that stay for a while and then leave. Objects are like relatives who move in and stay past their welcome." Daniel Gilbert, psychologist from Harvard University.

Economic and psychological research shows we are happier buying brief experiences on vacation rather than buying stuff to wear so give yourself freedom to spend on experiences knowing that the value you get back is many many times over.

Make saving money a game

There's one day a year where all the thrift shops where me and my family live sell everything there for a $1. My wife and I hold a contest where we take $5 and buy an entire outfit for each other. Whoever's outfit is liked more wins. We also look online to see whose outfit would have cost more to buy new. This year, my wife even snagged me an Armani coat for $1. I liked the coat when she showed it to me, but when I found out it was $500 new; I liked it and wore it a lot more.

Quadruple your money

Every-time you want to spend money, imagine it quadrupled. So the $10 you want to spend is actually $40. Now imagine that what you want to buy is four times the price. Do you still want it? If yes, go enjoy. If not, you've just saved yourself money, know you can choose to invest it in a way that quadruples or allocate it to something you really want to give you a greater return.

Understand what having unlimited amounts of money to spend in New York actually looks like

Let's look at what it would be like to have unlimited amounts of money to spend on your trip to New York.

Isolation

You take a private jet to your private New York hotel. There you are lavished with the best food, drink, and entertainment. Spending vast amounts of money on vacation equals being isolated.

If you're on your honeymoon and you want to be alone with your Amore, this is wonderful, but it can be equally wonderful to make new friends. Know this a study 'carried out by Brigham Young University, Utah found that while obesity increased risk of death by 30%, loneliness increased it by half.'

Comfort

Money can buy you late check outs of five-star hotels and priority boarding on airlines, all of which add up to comfort. But as this book has shown you, saving money in New York doesn't minimize comfort, that's just a lie travel agencies littered with glossy brochures want you to believe.

You can do late-check outs for free with the right credit cards and priority boarding can be purchased with a lot of airlines from $4. If you want to go big with first-class or business, flights offset your own travel costs by renting your own home or you can upgrade at the airport often for a fraction of what you would have paid booking a business flight online.

MORE TIPS TO FIND CHEAP FLIGHTS

"The use of travelling is to regulate imagination by reality, and instead of thinking how things may be, to see them as they are." Samuel Jackson

If you're working full-time, you can save yourself a lot of money by requesting your time off from work starting in the middle of the week. Tuesdays and Wednesdays are the cheapest days to fly. You can save thousands just by adjusting your time off.

The simplest secret to booking cheap flights is open parameters. Let's say you want to fly from Chicago to Paris. You enter the USA in from and select France under to. You may find flights from New York City to Paris for $70. Then you just need to find a cheap flight to NYC. Make sure you calculate full costs, including if you need airport accommodation and of course getting to and from airports, **but in nearly every instance open parameters will save you at least half the cost of the flight.**

If you're not sure about where you want to go, use open parameters to show you the cheapest destinations from your city. Start with skyscanner.net they include the low-cost airlines that others like Kayak leave out. Google Flights can also show you cheap destinations. To see these leave the WHERE TO section blank.

Open parameters can also show you the cheapest dates to fly. If you're flexible, you can save up to 80% of the flight cost. Always check the weather at your destination before you book. Sometimes a $400 flight will be $20, because it's monsoon season. But hey, if you like the rain, why not?

ALWAYS USE A PRIVATE BROWSER TO BOOK FLIGHTS

Skyscanner and other sites track your IP address and put prices up and down based on what they determine your strength of conviction to buy. e.g. if you've booked one-way and are looking for the return, these sites will jack the prices up by in most cases 50%. Incognito browsing pays.

Use a VPN such as Hola to book your flight from your destination

Install Hola, change your destination to the country you are flying to. The location from which a ticket is booked can affect the price significantly as algorithms consider local buying power.

Choose the right time to buy your ticket.

Choose the right time to buy your ticket, as purchasing tickets on a Sunday has been proven to be cheaper. If you can only book during the week, try to do it on a Tuesday.

Mistake fares

Email alerts from individual carriers are where you can find the best 'mistake fares". This is where a computer error has resulted in an airline offering the wrong fare. In my ex-perience, it's best to sign up to individual carriers email lists, but if you ARE lazy Secret Flying puts together a daily roster of mistake fares. Visit https://www.secretflying.com/errorfare/ to see if there're any errors that can benefit you.

Fly late for cheaper prices

Red-eye flights, the ones that leave later in the day, are typically cheaper and less crowded, so aim to book that flight if possible. You will also get through the airport much quicker at the end of the day. Just make sure there's ground transport available for when you land. You don't want to save $50 on the airfare and spend it on a taxi to your accommodation.

Use this APP for same day flights

If your plans are flexible, use 'Get The Flight Out' (http://www.gtfoflights.com/) a fare tracker Hopper that shows you same-day deeply discounted flights. This is best for long-haul flights with major carriers. You can often find a British Airways round-trip from JFK Airport to Heathrow for $300. If you booked this in advance, you'd pay at least double.

Take an empty water bottle with you

Airport prices on food and drinks are sky high. It disgusts me to see some airports charging $10 for a bottle of water. ALWAYS take an empty water bottle with you. It's relatively unknown, but most airports have drinking water fountains past the security check. Just type in your airport name to wateratairports.com to locate the fountain. Then once you've passed security (because they don't allow you to take 100ml or more of liquids) you can freely refill your bottle with water.

Round-the-World (RTW) Tickets

It is always cheaper to book your flights using a DIY approach. First, you may decide you want to stay longer in one country, and a RTW will charge you a hefty fee for changing your flight. Secondly, it all depends on where and when you travel and as we have discussed, there are many ways to ensure you pay way less than $1,500 for a year of flights. If you're travelling long-haul, the best strategy is to buy a return ticket, say New York, to Bangkok and then take cheap flights or transport around Asia and even to Australia and beyond.

Cut your costs to and from airports

Don't you hate it when getting to and from the airport is more expensive than your flight! And this is true in so many cities, especially European ones. For some reason, Google often shows the most expensive options. Use Omio to compare the cheapest transport options and save on airport transfer costs.

Car sharing instead of taxis

Check if New York has car sharing at the airport. Often they'll be tons of cars parked at the airport that are half the price of taking a taxi into the city. In most instances, you register your driving licence on an app and scan the code on the car to get going.

Checking Bags

Sometimes you need to check bags. If you do, put an Air-Tag inside. That way, you'll be about to see when you land where your bag is. This saves you the nail biting wait at baggage claim. And if worse comes to worst, and you see your bag is actually in another city, you can calmly stroll over to customer services and show them where your bag is.

Is it cheaper and more convenient to send your bags ahead?

Before you check your bags, check if it's cheaper to send them ahead of you with sendmybag.com obviously if you're staying in an Airbnb, you'll need to ask the hosts permission or you can time them to arrive the day after you. Hotels are normally very amenable.

What Credit Card Gives The Best Air Miles?

You can slash the cost of flights just for spending on a piece of plastic.

LET'S TALK ABOUT DEBT

Before we go into the best cards for each country, let's first talk about debt. The US system offers the best and biggest rewards. Why? Because they rely on the fact that many people living in the US will not pay their cards in full and the card will earn the bank significant interest payments. Other countries have a very different attitude towards money, debt, and saving than Americans. Thus in Germany and Austria the offerings aren't as favourable as the UK, Spain and Australia, where debt culture is more widely embraced. The takeaway here is this: **Only spend on one of these cards when you have set-up an automatic total monthly balance repayment. Don't let banks profit from your lizard brain!**

The best air-mile credit cards for those living in the UK

Amex Preferred Rewards Gold comes out top for those living in the UK for 2023.

Here are the benefits:

- 20,000-point bonus on £3,000 spend in first three months. These can be used towards flights with British Airways, Virgin Atlantic, Emirates and Etihad, and often

other rewards, such as hotel stays and car hire.
- 1 point per £1 spent
- 1 point = 1 airline point
- Two free visits a year to airport lounges
- No fee in year one, then £140/yr

The downside:

- Fail to repay fully and it's 59.9% rep APR interest, incl fee

You'll need to cancel before the £140/yr fee kicks in year two if you want to avoid it.

The best air-mile credit cards for those living in Canada

Aeroplan is the superior rewards program in Canada. The card has a high earn rate for Aeroplan Points, generating 1.5 points per $1 spent on eligible purchases. Look at the specifics of the eligible purchases https://www.aircanada.com/ca/en/aco/home/aeroplan/earn.html. If you're not spending on these things AMEX's Membership Rewards program offers you the best returns in Canada.

The best air-mile credit cards for those living in Germany

If you have a German bank account, you can apply for a Lufthansa credit card.

Earn 50,000 award miles if you spend $3,000 in purchases and paying the annual fee, both within the first 90 days.

Earn 2 award miles per $1 spent on ticket purchases directly from Miles & More integrated airline partners.

Earn 1 award mile per $1 spent on all other purchases.

The downsides

the €89 annual fee

Limited to fly with Lufthansa and its partners but you can capitalise on perks like the companion pass and airport lounge vouchers.

You need excellent credit to get this card.

The best air-mile credit cards for those living in Austria

"In Austria, Miles & More offers you a special credit card. You get miles for each purchase with the credit card. The Miles & More program calculates miles earned based on the distance flown and booking class. For European flights, the booking class is a flat rate. For intercontinental flights, mileage is calculated by multiplying the booking class by the distance flown." They offer a calculator so you can see how many points you could earn: https://www.miles-and-more.com/at/en/earn/airlines/mileage-calculator.html

The best air-mile credit cards for those living in Spain:

"The American Express card is the best known and oldest to earn miles, thanks to its membership Rewards program. When making payments with this card, points are added, which can then be exchanged for miles from airlines such as Iberia, Air Europa, Emirates or Alitalia." More information is available here: https://www.americanexpress.com/es-es/

The best air-mile credit cards for those living in Australia

ANZ Rewards Black comes out top for 2023.

180,000 bonus ANZ Reward Points (can get an $800 gift card) and $0 annual fee for the first year with the ANZ Rewards Black
Points Per Spend: 1 Velocity point on purchases of up to

$5,000 per statement period and 0.5 Velocity points thereafter.

Annual Fee: $0 in the first year, then $375 after.

Ns no set minimum income required, however, there is a minimum credit limit of $15,000 on this card.

Here are some ways you can hack points onto this card: https://www.pointhacks.com.au/credit-cards/anz-rewards-black-guide/

The best air-mile credit card solution for those living in the USA with a POOR credit score

The downside to Airline Mile cards is that they require good or excellent credit scores, meaning 690 or higher.

If you have bad credit and want to use credit card air lines you will need to rebuild your credit poor. The Credit One Bank® Platinum Visa® for Rebuilding Credit is a good credit card for people with bad credit who don't want to place a deposit on a secured card. The Credit One Platinum Visa offers a $300 credit limit, rewards, and the potential for credit-limit increases, which in time will help rebuild your score.

PLEASE don't sign-up for any of these cards if you can't trust yourself to repay it in full monthly. This will only lead to stress for you.

Frequent Flyer Memberships

"Points" and "miles" are often used interchangeably, but they're usually two very different things. Maximise and diversify your rewards by utilising both.

A frequent-flyer program (FFP) is a loyalty program offered by an airline. They are designed to encourage airline customers to fly more to accumulate points (also called miles, kilometres, or segments) which can be redeemed for air travel or other rewards.

You can sign up with any FFP program for free. There are three major airline alliances in the world: Oneworld, SkyTeam and Star Alliance. I am with One World https://www.oneworld.com/members because the points can be accrued and used for most flights.

The best return on your points is to use them for international business or first class flights with lie-flat seats. You would need 3 times more miles compared to an economy flight, but if you paid cash, you'd pay 5 - 10 times more than the cost of the economy flight, so it really pays to use your points only for upgrades. The worst value for your miles is to buy an economy seat or worse, a gift from the airlines gift-shop.

Sign up for a family/household account to pool miles together. If you share a common address, you can claim the miles with most airlines. You can use AwardWallet to keep track of your miles. Remember that they only last for 2 years, so use them before they expire.

How to get 70% off a Cruise

An average cruise can set you back $4,000. If you dream of cruising the oceans, but find the pricing too high, look at repositioning cruises. You can save as much as 70% by taking a cruise which takes the boat back to its home port.

These one-way itineraries take place during low cruise seasons when ships have to reposition themselves to locations where there's warmer weather.

To find a repositioning cruise, go to vacationstogo.com/repositioning_cruises.cfm. This simple and often overlooked booking trick is great for avoiding long flights with children and can save you so much money!

It's worth noting we don't have any affiliations with any travel service or provider. The links we suggest are chosen based on our experience of finding the best deals.

Pack like a Pro

"He who would travel happily must travel light." – Antoine de St. Exupery 59.

Travel as lightly as you can. We always need less than we think. You will be very grateful that you have a light pack when changing trains, travelling through the airport, catching a bus, walking to your accommodation, or climbing stairs.

Make a list of what you will wear for 7 days and take only those clothes. You can easily wash your things while you're travelling if you stay in an Airbnb with a washing machine or visit a local laundrette. Roll your clothes for maximum space usage and fewer wrinkles. If you feel really nervous about travelling with such few things, make sure you have a dressier outfit, a little black dress for women is always valuable, a shirt for men. Then pack shorts, a long pair of pants, loose tops and a hoodie to snuggle in. Remind yourself that a lack of clothing options is an opportunity to find bargain new outfits in thrift stores. You can either sell these on eBay after you've worn them or post them home to yourself. You'll feel less stressed, as you don't have to look after or feel weighed down by excess baggage. Here are three things to remember when packing:

- Co-ordinate colours - make sure everything you bring can be worn together.

- Be happy to do laundry - fresh clothes when you're travelling feels very luxurious.

- Take liquid minis no bigger than 60ml. Liquid is heavy, and you simply don't need to carry so much at one time.

- Buy reversible clothes (coats are a great idea), dresses which can be worn multiple different ways.

Checks to Avoid Fees

Always have 6 months' validity on your passport

To enter most countries, you need 6 months from the day you land. Factor in different time zones around the world if your passport is on the edge. Airport security will stop you from boarding your flight at the airport if your passport has 5 months and 29 days left.

Google Your Flight Number before you leave for the airport

Easily find out where your plane is from anywhere. Confirm the status of your flight before you leave for the airport with flightaware.com. This can save you long unnecessary wait times.

Check-in online

The founder, Ryan O'Leary of budget airline Ryanair famously said: "We think they should pay €60 for [failing to check-in online] being so stupid.". Always check-in online, even for international flights. Cheaper international carriers like Scoot will charge you at the airport to check-in.

Checking Bags

Never, ever check a bag if you can avoid it. Sometimes you need to check bags. If you do, put an AirTag inside. That way, you'll be about to see when you land where your bag is. This saves you the nail biting wait at baggage claim. And if worse comes to worst, and you see your bag is actually in another city, you can calmly stroll over to customer services and show them where your bag is.

Is it cheaper and more convenient to send your bags ahead?

Before you check your bags, check if it's cheaper to send them ahead of you with sendmybag.com obviously if you're staying in an Airbnb, you'll need to ask the hosts permission or you can time them to arrive the day after you. Hotels are normally very amenable.

It is always cheaper to put heavier items on a ship, rather than take them on a flight with you. Find the best prices for shipping at https://www.parcelmonkey.com/delivery-services/shipping-heavy-items

Use a fragile sticker

Put a 'Fragile' sticker on anything you check to ensure that it's handled better as it goes through security. It'll also be one of the first bags released after the flight, getting you out of the airport quicker.

If you check your bag, photograph it

Take a photo of your bag before you check it. This will speed up the paperwork if it is damaged or lost.

Relaxing at the Airport

The best way to relax at the airport is in a lounge where they provide free food, drinks, comfortable chairs, luxurious amenities (many have showers) and, if you're lucky, a peaceful ambience. If you're there for a longer time, look for Airport Cubicles, sleep pods which charge by the hour.

You can use your FFP Card (Frequent Flyer Memberships) to get into select lounges for free. Check your eligibility before you pay.

If you're travelling a lot, I'd recommend investing in a Priority Pass for the airport.

It includes 850-plus airport lounges around the world. The cost is $99 for the year and $27 per lounge visit or you can pay $399 for the year all inclusive.

If you need a lounge for a one-off day, you can get a Day Pass. Buy it online for a discount, it always works out cheaper than buying at the airport. Use www.LoungePass.com.

Lounges are also great if you're travelling with kids, as they're normally free for kids and will definitely cost you less than snacks for your little ones. The rule is that kids should be seen and not heard, so consider this before taking an overly excited child who wants to run around, or you might be asked to leave even after you've paid.

Money: How to make it, spend it and save it while travelling

How to earn money WHILE travelling

"Twenty years from now you will be more disappointed by the things you didn't do than by the ones you did do. So throw off the bowlines. Sail away from the safe harbour." - H. Jackson Brown

Digital nomads receive a lot of hype. Put simply, they are " professionals who work online and therefore don't need to tie themselves to one particular office, city, or even country."

The first step in becoming a digital nomad, earning money while travelling, is knowing what you can offer. Your market is the entire world. So, what product or service would you like to offer that they would pay for? Take some time to think about this. In German, they say you should do whatever comes easily to your hand. For example, I've always loved finding bargains, it comes easily to me. Yet I studied Law and Finance at University, which definitely did not come easy. It's not a shock that it didn't transpire into a career. And served more as a lesson in not following my ego.

There are thousands of possibilities to generate income while travelling; offering services like tutorial, coaching, writing service, PR, blogging. Most travellers I meet try their hand at blogging and earning from the advertisements. This is great if you have some savings, but if you need to earn straight away to travel, this should be on the back burner, as it takes time to establish. Still, if this comes easily to you, do it!

You want to make good money fast. Ask yourself, what is it you are good at and how can you deliver maximum value to other people? Here are some ideas if you're totally dum-founded:

Teaching English online - you will need a private room for this. Be aware that if you're from the USA and the country you want to work in requires a federal-level background check, it may take months, so apply early. Opportunities are on: t.vipkid.com.cn, abc360.com, italki.com, ver-balplanet.com and verbling.com. You can expect to earn $20 an hour.

Work in a hostel. Normally you'll get some cash and free accommodation.

Fruit picking. I picked Bananas in Tully, Australia for $20 an hour. The jobs are menial but can be quite meditative. Look on WWOOF.org for organic farm work. There are also amazing opportunities on worldpacker.com and work-away.com

fiverr.com - offer a small service, like making a video tem-plate and changing the content for each buyer.

Do freelance work online: marketing, finance, writing, App creation, graphic designer, UX or UI designer, SEO opti-miser / expert. Create a profile on upwork.com - you need to put in a lot of work to make this successful, but if you have a unique skill like coding or marketing, it can be very lucrative.

Make a udemy.com course. Can you offer a course in something people will pay for? e.g. stock trading, knitting or marketing.

Use Skype to deliver all manner of services: language lessons, therapy, coaching etc. Google for what you could offer. Most specialisms have a platform you can use to find clients and they will take a cut of your earnings/ require a fee.

You could work on luxury yachts in the med. It's hard work, but you can save money - DesperateSailors.com

Become an Airbnb experience host - but this requires you to know one place and stay there for a time. And you will need a work visa for that country.

Work on a cruise ship. This isn't a digital nomad job but it will help you travel and save at the same time.

Rent your place out on Airbnb while you travel and get a cleaner to manage it. The easiest solution if you own or have a long-term rent contract.

Passive Income Ideas that earn $1000+ a month

- Start a YouTube Channel.

- Start a Membership Website.

- Write a Book.

- Create a Lead Gen Website for Service Businesses.

- Join the Amazon Affiliate Program.

- Market a Niche Affiliate Opportunity.

- Create an Online Course.

- Invest in Real Estate

-

How to spend money

Bank ATM fees vary from $2.50 per transaction to as high as $5 or more, depending on the ATM and the country. You can completely skip those fees by paying with card and using a card which can hold multiple currencies.

Budget travel hacking begins with a strategy to spend without fees. Your individual strategy depends on the country you legally reside in as to what cards are available. Happily there are some fin-tech solutions which can save you thousands on those pesky ATM withdrawal fees and are widely available globally. Here are a selection of cards you can pre-charge with currency for New York:

N26

N26 is a 12-year-old digital bank. I have been using them for over 6 years. The key advantage is fee-free card transactions abroad. They have a very elegant app, where you can check your timeline for all transactions listed in real time or manage your in-app security anywhere. The card you receive is a Mastercard so you can use it everywhere. If you lose the card, you don't have to call anyone, just open the app and swipe 'lock card'. It puts your purchases into a graph automatically so you can see what you spend on. You can open an account from abroad entirely online, all you need is your passport and a camera n26.com

Revolut

Revolut is a multi-currency account that allows you to hold and exchange 29 currencies and spend fee-free abroad. It's a UK based neobank, but accepts customers from all over the world.

Wise debit card

If you're going to be in one place for a long time,
the Wise debit card is like having your travel money on a
card – it lets you spend money at the real exchange rate.

Monzo

Monzo is good if your UK based. They offer a fee-free UK
account. Fee-free international money transfers and fee-
free spending abroad.

The downside

The cards above are debit cards, meaning you need to
have money in those accounts to spend it. This comes with
one big downside: safety. Credit card issuers' have "zero
liability" meaning you're not liable for unauthorised
charges. All the cards listed above do provide cover for
unauthorised charges but times vary greatly in how quickly
you'd get your money back if it were stolen.

The best option is to check in your country to see which credit cards are the best for travelling and set up monthly payments to repay the whole amount so you don't pay unnecessary interest. In the USA, Schwab regularly ranks at the top for travel credit cards. Credit cards are always the safer option when abroad simply because you get your money back faster if its stolen and if you're renting cars, most will give you free insurance when you book the car rental using the card, saving you money.

Always withdraw money; never exchange.

Money exchanges, whether they be on the streets or in the airports will NEVER give you a good exchange rate. Do not bring bundles of cash. Instead, withdraw local currency from the ATM as needed and try to use only free ATMs. Many in airports charge you a fee to withdraw cash. Look for bigger ATMs attached to banks to avoid this.

Recap

- Take cash from local, non-charging ATMs for the best rates.

- Never change at airport exchange desks unless you absolutely have to, then just change just enough to be able get to a bank ATM.

- Bring a spare credit card for emergencies.

- Split cash in various places on your person (pockets, shoes) and in your luggage. It's never sensible to keep your cash or cards all in one place.

- In higher risk areas, use a money belt under your clothes or put $50 in your shoe or bra.

Revolut

Revolut is a multi-currency account that allows you to hold and exchange 29 currencies and spend fee-free abroad. It's a UK based neobank, but accepts customers from all over the world.

Wise debit card
If you're going to be in one place for a long time the Wise debit card is like having your travel money on a card – it lets you spend money at the real exchange rate.

Monzo
Monzo is good if your UK based. They offer a fee-free UK account. Fee-free international money transfers and fee-free spending abroad.

The downside

The cards above are debit cards, meaning you need to have money in those accounts to spend it. This comes with one big downside: safety. Credit card issuers' have "zero liability" meaning you're not liable for unauthorised charges. All of the cards listed above do provide cover for unauthorised charges but times vary greatly in how quickly you'd get your money back if it were stolen.

The best option is to check in your country to see which credit cards are the best for travelling and set up monthly payments to repay the whole amount so you don't pay un-necessary interest. In the USA, Schwab[2] regularly ranks at the top for travel credit cards. Credit cards are always the safer option when abroad simply because you get your money back faster if its stolen and if you're renting cars, most will give you free insurance when you book the car rental using the card, saving you money.

---

[2] Charles Schwab High Yield Checking accounts refund every single ATM fee worldwide, require no minimum balance and have no monthly fee.

Always withdraw money; never exchange.

Money exchanges whether they be on the streets or in the airports will NEVER give you a good exchange rate. Do not bring bundles of cash. Instead withdraw local currency from the ATM as needed and try to use only free ATM's. Many in airports charge you a fee to withdraw cash. Look for bigger ATM's attached to banks to avoid this.

Recap

- Take cash from local, non-charging ATMs for the best rates.
- Never change at airport exchange desks unless you absolutely have to, then just change just enough to be able get to a bank ATM.
- Bring a spare credit card for emergencies.
- Split cash in various places on your person (pockets, shoes) and in your luggage. Its never sensible to keep your cash or cards all in one place.
- In higher risk areas, use a money belt under your clothes or put $50 in your shoe or bra.

How to save money while travelling

Saving money while travelling sounds like an oxymoron, but it can be done with little to no effort. Einstein is credited as saying, "Compound interest is the eighth wonder of the world." If you saved and invested $100 today, in 20 years, it would be $2,000 thanks to the power of compound interest. It makes sense then to save your money, invest and make even more money.

The Acorns app is a simple system for this. It rounds up your credit card purchases and puts the rest into a savings account. So if you pay for a coffee and its $3.01, you'll save 0.99 cents. You won't even notice you're saving by using this app: www.acorns.com

Here are some more generic ways you can always save money while travelling:

Device Safety

Having your phone, iPad or laptop stolen is one BIG and annoying way you can lose money travelling. The simple solution is to use apps to track your devices. Some OSes have this feature built-in. Prey will try your smartphones or laptops (preyproject.com).

Book New Airbnb's

When you take a risk on a new Airbnb listing, you save money. Just make sure the hosts profile is at least 3 years old and has reviews.

If you end up in an overcrowded city

The website https://campspace.com/ is like Airbnb for camping in people's garden and is a great way to save money if you end up in a city during a big event.

Look out for free classes

Lots of hostels offer free classes for guests. If you're planning to stay in a hostel, check out what classes your hostel offers. I have learnt languages, cooking techniques, dance styles, drawing and all manner of things for free by taking advantage of free classes at hostels.

Get student discounts

If you're studying buy an ISIC card - International Student Identity Card. It is internationally recognised, valid in 133 countries and offers more than 150,000 discounts!

Get Senior Citizen discounts

Most state run attractions, ie, museums, galleries will offer a discount for people over 65 with ID.

Instal maps.me

Maps me is extremely good for travelling without data. It's like offline google maps without the huge download size.

Always buy travel insurance

Don't travel without travel insurance. It is a small cost to pay compared with what could be a huge medical bill.

Travel Apps That'll Make Budget Travel Easier

Travel apps are useful for booking and managing travel logistics. They have one fatal downside: they can track you in the app and keep prices up. If you face this, access the site from an incognito browser tab.

Here are the best apps and what they can do for you:

- Best For flight Fare-Watching: Hopper.

- Best for booking flights: Skyscanner and Google Flights

- Best for timing airport arrivals: FlightAware - check on delays, cancellations and gate changes.

- Best for overcoming a fear of flying: SkyGuru - turbulence forecasts for the route you're flying.

- Best for sharing your location: TripWhistle - text or send your GPS coordinates or location easily.

- Best for splitting expenses among co-travellers: Splittr, Trip Splitter, Venmo or Splitwise.

How NOT to be ripped off

"One of the great things about travel is that you find out ho
w many good, kind people there are."
— Edith Wharton

The quote above may seem ill placed in a chapter entitled
how not to be ripped off, but I included it to remind you
that the vast majority of people do not want to rip you off.
In fact, scammers are normally limited to three situations:

1.   Around heavily visited attractions - these places are
      targeted purposively due to sheer footfall. Many
      criminals believe ripping people off is simply a num-
      bers game.

2.   In cities or countries with low-salaries or communist
      ideologies. If they can't make money in the country,
      they seek to scam foreigners. If you have travelled to
      India, Morocco or Cuba you will have observed this
      phenomenon.

3.   When you are stuck and the person helping you
      know you have limited options.

Scammers know that most people will avoid confrontation.
Don't feel bad about utterly ignoring someone and saying
no. Here are six strategies to avoid being ripped off:

1.   Never ever agree to pay as much as you want. Always decide on a price before.

Whoever you're dealing with is trained to tell you, they are
uninterested in money. This is a trap. If you let people do

this they will ask for MUCH MORE money at the end, and because you have used there service, you will feel obliged to pay. This is a conman's trick and nothing more.

2. Pack light

You can move faster and easier. If you take heavy luggage, you will end up taking taxis which are comparatively very costly over time.

3. NEVER use the airport taxi service. Plan to use public transport before you reach the airport.

4. Don't buy a sim card from the airport. Buy from the local supermarkets it will cost 50% less.

5. Eat at local restaurants serving regional food

Food defines culture. Exploring all delights available to the palate doesn't need to cost enormous sums.

6. Ask the locals what something should cost, and try not to pay over that.

7. If you find yourself with limited options. e.g. your taxi dumps you on the side of the road because you refuse to pay more (common in India and parts of South America) don't act desperate and negotiate as if you have other options or you will be extorted.

8. Don't blindly rely on social media[3]

Let's say you post in a Facebook group that you want tips for travelling to The Maldives. A lot of the comments you will receive come from guides, hosts and restaurants doing their own promotion. It's estimated that 50% or more of

---

[3] https://arstechnica.com/tech-policy/2019/12/social-media-plat-forms-leave-95-of-reported-fake-accounts-up-study-finds/

Facebook's current monthly active users are fake. And what's worse, a recent study found Social media platforms leave 95% of reported fake accounts up. These accounts are the digital versions of the men who hang around the Grand Palace in Bangkok telling tourists its closed, to divert you to shops where they will receive a commission for bringing you.

It can also be the case that genuine comments come from people who have totally different interests, beliefs and yes, budgets to yours. Make your experience your own and don't believe every comment you read.

Bottom line: use caution when accepting recommendations on social media and always fact-check with your own research.

Small tweaks on the road add up to big differences in your bank balance

Take advantage of other hotel amenities

If you fancy a swim but you're nowhere near the ocean, try the nearest hotel with a pool. As long as you buy a drink, the hotel staff will probably grant you access.

Fill up your mini bar for free.

Fill up your mini bar for free by storing things from the breakfast bar or grocery shop in your mini bar to give you a greater selection of drinks and food without the hefty price tag.

Save yourself some ironing

Use the steam from the shower to get rid of wrinkles in clothing. If something is creased, leave it trapped with the steam in the bathroom overnight for even better results.

See somewhere else for free

Opt for long stopovers, allowing you to experience another city without spending much money.

Wear your heaviest clothes

On the plane to save weight in your pack, allowing you to bring more with you. Big coats can then be used as pillows to make your flight more comfortable.

Don't get lost while you're away.

Find where you want to go using Google Maps, then type 'OK Maps' into the search bar to store this information for offline viewing.

Use car renting services

Share Now or Car2Go allow you to hire a car for 2 hours for $25 in a lot of European countries.

Share Rides

Use sites like blablacar.com to find others who are driving in your direction. It can be 80% cheaper than normal transport. Just check the drivers reviews.

Use free gym passes

Get a free gym day pass by googling the name of a local gym and free day pass.

When asked by people providing you a service where you are from..

If there's no price list for the service you are asking for, when asked where you are from, Say you are from a lesser-known poorer country. I normally say Macedonia, and if they don't know where it is, add it's a poor country. If you say UK, USA, the majority of Europe bar the well-known poorer countries taxi drivers, tour operators etc will match the price to what they think you pay at home.

Set-up a New Uber/ other car hailing app account for discounts

By googling you can find offers with $50 free for new users in most cities for Uber/ Lyft/ Bolt and alike. Just set up a new gmail.com email account to take advantage.

Where and How to Make Friends

"People don't take trips, trips take people." – John Steinbeck

Become popular at the airport

Want to become popular at the airport? Pack a power bar with multiple outlets and just see how many friends you can make. It's amazing how many people forget their chargers, or who packed them in the luggage that they checked in.

Stay in Hostels

First of all, Hostels don't have to be shared dorms, and they cater to a much wider demographic than is assumed. Hostels are a better environment for meeting people than hotels, and more importantly, they tended to open up excursion opportunities that further opened up that opportunity.

Or take up a hobby

If hostels are a definite no-no for you; find an interest. Take up a hobby where you will meet people. I've dived for years and the nature of diving is you're always paired up with a dive buddy. I met a lot of interesting people that way.

Small tweaks on the road add up to big differences in your bank balance

Take advantage of other hotel's amenities

If you fancy a swim but you're nowhere near the ocean, try the nearest hotel with a pool. As long as you buy a drink, the hotel staff will likely grant you access.

Fill up your mini bar for free.

Fill up your mini bar for free by storing things from the breakfast bar or grocery shop in your mini bar to give you a greater selection of drinks and food without the hefty price tag.

Save yourself some ironing

Use the steam from the shower to get rid of wrinkles in clothing. If something is creased, leave it trapped with the steam in the bathroom overnight for even better results.

See somewhere else for free

Opt for long stopovers, allowing you to experience another city without spending much money.

Wear your heaviest clothes

on the plane to save weight in your pack, allowing you to bring more with you. Big coats can then be used as pillows to make your flight more comfortable.

Don't get lost while you're away.

Find where you want to go using Google Maps, then type 'OK Maps' into the search bar to store this information for offline viewing.

Use car renting services

Share Now or Car2Go allow you to hire a car for 2 hours for $25 in a lot of Europe.

Share Rides

Use sites like blablacar.com to find others who are driving in your direction. It can be 80% cheaper than normal transport. Just check the drivers reviews.

Use free gym passes

Get a free gym day pass by googling the name of a local gym and free day pass.

When asked by people providing you a service where you are from..

If there's no price list for the service you are asking for, when asked where you are from, Say you are from a lesser-known poorer country. I normally say Macedonia, and if they don't know where it is, add it's a poor country. If you say UK, USA, the majority of Europe bar the well-known poorer countries taxi drivers, tour operators etc will match the price to what they think you pay at home.

Set-up a New Uber/ other car hailing app account for discounts

By googling you can find offers with $50 free for new users in most cities for Uber/ Lyft/ Bolt and alike. Just set up a new gmail.com email account to take advantage.

Where and How to Make Friends

"People don't take trips, trips take people." – John Steinbeck

Become popular at the airport

Want to become popular at the airport? Pack a power bar
with multiple outlets and just see how many friends you
can make. It's amazing how many people forget their
chargers, or who packed them in the luggage that they
checked in.

Stay in Hostels

First of all, Hostels don't have to be shared dorms, and
they cater to a much wider demographic than is assumed.
Hostels are a better environment for meeting people than
hotels, and more importantly they tended to open up excursion opportunities that further opened up that opportunity.

Or take up a hobby

If hostels are a definite no-no for you; find an interest. Take
up a hobby where you will meet people. I've dived for years
and the nature of diving is you're always paired up with a
dive buddy. I met a lot of interesting people that way.

When unpleasantries come your way...

We all have our good and bad days travelling, and on a bad day you can feel like just taking a flight home. Here are some ways to overcome common travel problems:

Anxiety when flying

It has been over 40 years since a plane has been brought down by turbulence. Repeat that number to yourself: 40 years! Planes are built to withstand lighting strikes, extreme storms and ultimately can adjust course to get out of their way. Landing and take-off are when the most accidents happen, but you have statistically three times the chance of winning a huge jackpot lottery, then you do of dying in a plane crash.

If you feel afraid on the flight, focus on your breathing saying the word 'smooth' over and over until the flight is smooth. Always check the airline safety record on airlinerating.com I was surprised to learn Ryanair and Easyjet as much less safe than Wizz Air according to those ratings because they sell similarly priced flights. If there is extreme turbulence, I feel much better knowing I'm in a 7 star safety plane.

Wanting to sleep instead of seeing new places

This is a common problem. Just relax, there's little point doing fun things when you feel tired. Factor in jet-lag to your travel plans. When you're rested and alert you'll enjoy your new temporary home much more. Many people hate the first week of a long-trip because of jet-lag and often blame this on their first destination, but its rarely true. Ask travellers who 'hate' a particular place and you will see that very often they either had jet-lag or an unpleasant journey there.

Going over budget

Come back from a trip to a monster credit card bill? Hopefully, this guide has prevented you from returning to an unwanted bill. Of course, there are costs that can creep up and this is a reminder about how to prevent them making their way on to your credit card bill:

- To and from the airport. Solution: leave adequate time and take the cheapest method - book before.

- Baggage. Solution: take hand luggage and post things you might need to yourself.

- Eating out. Solution: go to cheap eats places and suggest those to friends.

- Parking. Solution: use apps to find free parking

- Tipping. Solution Leave a modest tip and tell the server you will write them a nice review.

- Souvenirs. Solution: fridge magnets only.

- Giving to the poor. (This one still gets me, but if you're giving away $10 a day - it adds up) Solution: volunteer your time instead and recognise that in tourist destinations many beggars are run by organised crime gangs.

Price v Comfort

I love traveling. I don't love struggling. I like decent accommodation, being able to eat properly and see places and enjoy. I am never in the mood for low-cost airlines or crappy transfers, so here's what I do to save money.

- Avoid organised tours unless you are going to a place where safety is a real issue. They are expensive and constrain your wanderlust to typical things. I only recommend them in Algeria, Iran and Papua New Guinea - where language and gender views pose serious problems all cured by a reputable tour organiser.

- Eat what the locals do.

- Cook in your Airbnb/ hostel where restaurants are expensive.

- Shop at local markets.

- Spend time choosing your flight, and check the operator on arilineratings.com

- Mix up hostels and Airbnbs. Hostels for meeting people, Airbnb for relaxing and feeling 'at home'.

Not knowing where free toilets are

Use Toilet Finder - https://play.google.com/store/apps/details?id=com.bto.toilet&hl=en

Your Airbnb is awful

Airbnb customer service is notoriously bad. Help yourself out. Try to sort things out with the host, but if you can't, take photos of everything e.g bed, bathroom, mess, doors, contact them within 24 hours. Tell them you had to leave and pay for new accommodation. Ask politely for a full refund including booking fees. With photographic evidence and your new accommodation receipt, they can't refuse.

The airline loses your bag

Go to the Luggage desk before leaving the airport and report the bag missing. Hopefully you've headed the advice to put an AirTag in your checked bag and you can show them where to find your bag. Most airlines will give you an overnight bag, ask where you're staying and return the bag to you within three days. It's extremely rare for Airlines to lose your bag due to technological innovation, but if that happens you should submit an insurance claim after the three days is up, including receipts for everything you had to buy in the interim.

Your travel companion lets you down

Whether it's a breakup or a friend cancelling, it sucks and can ramp up costs. The easiest solution to finding a new travel companion is to go to a well-reviewed hostel and find someone you want to travel with. You should spend at least three days getting to know this person before you suggest travelling together. Finding someone in person is always better than finding someone online, because you can get a better idea of whether you will have a smooth journey together. Travel can make or break friendships.

Culture shock

I had one of the strongest culture shocks while spending 6 months in Japan. It was overwhelming how much I had to prepare when I went outside of the door (googling words and sentences what to use, where to go, which station and train line to use, what is this food called in Japanese and how does its look etc.). I was so tired constantly but in the end I just let go and went with my extremely bad Japanese. If you feel culture shocked its because your brain is referencing your surroundings to what you know. Stop comparing, have Google translate downloaded and relax.

Your Car rental insurance is crazy expensive

I always use carrentals.com and book with a credit card. Most credit cards will give you free insurance for the car, so you don't need to pay the extra. Some unsavoury companies will bump the price up when you arrive. Ask to speak to a manager. If this doesn't resolve, it google "consumer ombudsman for NAME OF COUNTRY." and seek an immediate full refund on the balance difference you paid. It is illegal in most countries to alter the price of a rental car when the person arrives to pickup a pre-arranged car.

A note on Car Rental Insurance

Always always always rent a car with a credit card that has rental vehicle coverage built into the card and is automatically applied when you rent a car. Then there's no need to buy additional rental insurance (check with your card on the coverage they protect some exclude collision coverage). Do yourself a favour when you step up to the desk to rent the car tell the agent you're already covered and won't be buying anything today. They work on commission and you'll save time and your patience avoiding the upselling.

You're sick

First off ALWAYS, purchase travel insurance. Including emergency transport up to $500k even to back home, which is usually less than $10 additional. I use https://www.comparethemarket.com/travel-insurance/ to find the best days. If I am sick I normally check into a hotel with room service and ride it out.

Make a Medication Travel Kit

Take travel sized medications with you:

- Antidiarrheal medication (for example, bismuth sub-salicylate, loperamide)

- Medicine for pain or fever (such as acetaminophen, aspirin, or ibuprofen)

- Throat Lozenges

Save yourself from most travel related hassles

- Do not make jokes with immigration and customs staff. A misunderstanding can lead to HUGE fines.

- Book the most direct flight you can find nonstop if possible.

- Carry a US$50 bill for emergency cash. I have entered a country and all ATM and credit card systems were down. US$ can be exchanged nearly anywhere in the world and is useful in extreme situations, but where possible don't exchange, as you will lose money.

- Check, and recheck, required visas and such BEFORE the day of your trip. Some countries, for instance, require a ticket out of the country in order to enter. Others, like the US and Australia, require electronic authorisation in advance.

- Airport security is asinine and inconsistent around the world. Keep this in mind when connecting flights. Always leave at least 2 hours for international connections or international to domestic. In Stansted for example, they force you to buy one of their plastic bags, and remove your liquids from your own plastic bag…. just to make money from you. And this adds to the time it will take to get through security, so lines are long.

- Wiki travel is perfect to use for a lay of the land.

- Expensive luggage rarely lasts longer than cheap luggage, in my experience. Fancy leather bags are toast with air travel.

Food

- When it comes to food, eat in local restaurants, not tourist-geared joints. Any place with the menu in three or more languages is going to be overpriced.

- Take a spork - a knife, spoon and fork all in one.

Water Bottle

Take a water bottle with a filter. We love these ones from Water to Go.

Empty it before airport security and separate the bottle and filter as some airport people will try and claim it has liquids…

Bug Sprays

If you're heading somewhere tropical spray your clothes with Permethrin before you travel. It lasts 40 washes and saves space in your bag. A 'Bite Away' zapper can be used after the bite to totally erase it. It cuts down on the itching and erases the bite from your skin.

Order free mini's

Don't buy those expensive travel sized toiletries, order travel sized freebies online. This gives you the opportunity to try brands you've never used before, and who knows, you might even find your new favourite soap.

Take a waterproof bag

If you're travelling alone you can swim without worrying about your phone, wallet and passport laying on the beach.

You can also use it as a source of entertainment on those ultra budget flights.

Make a private entertainment centre anywhere

Always take an eye-mask, earplugs, a scarf and a kindle reader - so you can sleep and entertain yourself anywhere!

The best Travel Gadgets

The door alarm

If you're nervous and staying in private rooms or airbnbs take a door alarm. For those times when you just don't feel safe, it can help you fall asleep. You can get tiny ones for less than $10 from Amazon: https://www.amazon.com/Travel-door-alarm/s?k=Travel+door+alarm

Smart Blanket

Amazon sells a 6 in 1 heating blanket that is very useful for cold plane or bus trips. Its great if you have poor circulation as it becomes a detachable Foot Warmer: Amazon http://amzn.to/2hTYlOP I paid $49.00.

The coat that becomes a tent

https://www.adiff.com/products/tent-jacket. This is great if you're going to be doing a lot of camping.

Clever Tank Top with Secret Pockets

Keep your valuables safe in this top. Perfect for all climates. https://www.amazon.com/Clever-Travel-Companion-Unisex-secret/dp/B00O94PXLE on Amazon for $39.90

Optical Camera Lens for Smartphones and Tablets

Leave your bulky camera at home. Turn your device into a high-performance camera. Buy on Amazon for $9.95

Travel-sized Wireless Router with USB Media Storage

Convert any wired network to a wireless network. Buy on Amazon for $17.99

Buy a Scrubba Bag to wash your clothes on the go

Or a cheaper imitable. You can wash your clothes on the go.

Hacks for Families

Rent an Airbnb apartment so you can cook

Apartments are much better for families, as you have all the amenities you'd have at home. They are normally cheaper per person too. We are the first travel guide publisher to include Airbnb's in our recommendations if you think any of these need updating you can email me at philgtang@gmail.com

Shop at local markets

Eat seasonal products and local products. Get closer to the local market and observe the prices and the offer. What you can find more easily, will be the cheapest.

Take Free Tours

Download free podcast tours of the destination you are visiting. The podcast will tell you where to start, where to go, and what to look for. Often you can find multiple podcast tours of the same place. Listen to all of them if you like, each one will tell you a little something new.

Pack Extra Ear Phones

If you go on a museum tour, they often have audio guides. Instead of having to rent one for each person, take some extra earphones. Most audio tour devices have a place to plug in a second set.

Buy Souvenirs Ahead of Time

If you are buying souvenirs somewhere touristy, you are paying a premium price. By ordering the same exact products online, you can save a lot of money.

Use Cheap Transportation

Do as the locals do, including weekly passes.

Carry Reusable Water Bottles

Spending money on water and other beverages can quickly add up. Instead of paying for drinks, take some refillable water bottles.

Combine Attractions

Many major cities offer ticket bundles where one price gets you into 5 or 6 popular attractions. You will need to plan ahead of time to decide what things you plan to do on vacation and see if they are selling these activities together.

Pack Snacks

Granola bars, apples, baby carrots, bananas, cheese crackers, juice boxes, pretzels, fruit snacks, apple sauce, grapes, and veggie chips.

Stick to Carry-On Bags

Do not pay to check a large bag. Even a small child can pull a carry-on.

Visit free art galleries and museums

Just google the name + free days.

Eat Street Food

There's a lot of unnecessary fear around this. You can watch the food prepared. Go for the stands that have a steady queue.

Travel Gadgets for Families

Dropcam

Are what-if scenarios playing out in your head? Then you need Dropcam.

'Dropcam HD Internet Wi-Fi Video Monitoring Cameras help you watch what you love from anywhere. In less than a minute, you'll have it setup and securely streaming video to you over your home Wi-Fi. Watch what you love while away with Dropcam HD.'

Approximate Price: $139

Kelty-Child-Carrier

Voted as one of the best hiking essentials if you're traveling with kids and can carry a child up to 18kg.

Jetkids Bedbox

No more giving up your own personal space on the plane with this suitcase that becomes a bed.

Safety

"If you think adventure is dangerous, try routine. It's lethal." – Paulo Coelho

Backpacker murdered is a media headline that leads people to think traveling is more dangerous than it is. The media sensationalise the rare murders and deaths of backpackers and travellers. The actual chances of you dying abroad are extremely extremely low.

Let's take the USA as an example. In 2018, 724 Americans **died** from unnatural causes, 167 died from car accidents, while the majority of the other deaths resulted from drownings, suicides, and non-vehicular accidents. Contrast this with the 15,000 murders in the US in 2018, and travelling abroad looks much safer than staying at home.

There are many things you can to keep yourself safe. Here are our tips.

1. Always check fco.co.uk before travelling. NEVER RELY on websites or books. Things are changing constantly and the FCO's (UK's foreign office) advice is always UP TO DATE (hourly) and **extremely conservative**.

2. Check your mindset. I've travelled alone to over 180 countries and the main thing I learnt is if you walk around scared, or anticipating you're going to be pickpocketed, your constant fear will attract bad energy. Murders or attacks on travellers are the mainstay of media, not reality, especially in countries familiar with travellers. The only place I had cause to genuinely fear for my life was Papua New Guinea -

where nothing actually happened to me only my own panic over culture shock.

There are many things you can do to stop yourself being victim to the two main problems when travelling: theft or being scammed.

I will address theft first. Here are my top tips:

- Stay alert while you're out and always have an exit strategy.

- Keep your money in a few different places on your person and your passport somewhere it can't be grabbed.

- Take a photo of your passport on your phone in case. If you do lose it, google for your embassy, you can usually get a temporary pretty fast.

- Google safety tips for travelling in your country to help yourself out and memorise the emergency number.

- At hostels, keep your large bag in the room far under the bed/out of the way with a lock on the zipper.

- On buses/trains, I would even lock my bag to the luggage rack.

- Get a personal keychain alarm. The sound will scare anyone away.

- Don't wear any jewellery. A man attempted to rob a friend of her engagement ring in Bogota, Colombia, and in hindsight I wished I'd told her to leave it at home/wear it on a hidden necklace, as the chaos it created was avoidable.

- Don't turn your back to traffic while you use your phone.

- When travelling in the tuktuk sit in the middle and keep your bag secure. Wear sunglasses as dust can easily get in your eyes.

- Don't let anyone give you flowers, bracelets, or any type of trinket, even if they insist it's for free and compliment you like crazy.

- Don't let strangers know that you are alone - unless they are travel friends ;-)

- Lastly, and most importantly -Trust your gut! If it doesn't feel right, it isn't.

How I got hooked on budget travelling

'We're on holiday' is what my dad used to say to justify getting us in so much debt we lost our home and all our things when I was 11. We moved from the suburban bliss of Hemel Hempstead to a run down council estate in inner-city London, near my dad's new job as a refuge collector, a fancy word for dustbin man. I lost all my school friends while watching my dad go through a nervous breakdown.

My dad loved walking up a hotel lobby desk without a care in the world. So much so, that he booked overpriced holidays on credit cards. A lot of holidays. As it turned out, we couldn't afford any of them. In the end, my dad had no choice but to declare bankruptcy. When my mum realised, he'd racked up so much debt our family unit dissolved. A neat and perhaps as painless a summary of events that lead me to my life's passion: budget travel that doesn't compromise on fun, safety or comfort.

I started travelling full-time at the age of 18. I wrote the first Super Cheap Insider guide for friends visiting Norway - which I did for a month on less than $250. When sales reached 10,000 I decided to form the Super Cheap Insider Guides company. As I know from first-hand experience debt can be a noose around our necks, and saying 'oh come on, we're on vacation' isn't a get out of jail free card. In fact, its the reverse of what travel is supposed to bring you - freedom.

Before I embarked upon writing Super Cheap Insider guides, many, many people told me that my dream was impossible. Travelling on a budget could never be comfortable. I hope this guide has proved to you what I have known for a long-time: budget travel can feel luxurious when you know and use the insider hacks.

And apologies if I depressed you with my tale of woe. My dad is now happily remarried and works as a chef in London at a fancy hotel - the kind he used to take us to!

A final word...

There's a simple system you can use to think about budget travel. In life, we can choose two of the following: cheap, fast, or quality. So if you want it Cheap and fast you will get a lower quality service. Fast-food is the perfect example. The system holds true for purchasing anything while travelling. I always choose cheap and quality, except at times where I am really limited on time. Normally, you can make small tweaks to make this work for you. Ultimately, you must make choices about what's most important to you and heed your heart's desires.

'Your heart is the most powerful muscle in your body. Do what it says.' Jen Sincero

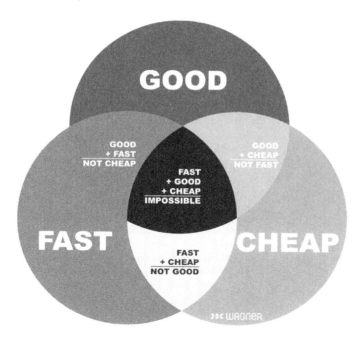

Our Writers

Phil Tang was born in London to Irish immigrant, Phil graduated from The London School of Economics with a degree in Law. Now he travels full-time in search of travel bargains with his wife, dog and a baby and a toddler.

Ali Blythe has been writing about amazing places for 17 years. He loves travel and especially tiny budgets equalling big adventures nearly as much as his family. He recently trekked the Satopanth Glacier trekking through those ways from where no one else would trek. Ali is an adventurer by nature and bargainist by religion.

Michele Whitter writes about languages and travel. What separates her from other travel writers is her will to explain complex topics in a no-nonsense, straightforward way. She doesn't promise the world. But always delivers step-by-step methods you can immediately implement to travel on a budget.

Lizzy McBraith, Lizzy's input on Super Cheap Insider Guides show you how to stretch your money further so you can travel cheaper, smarter, and with more wanderlust. She loves going over land on horses and helps us refine each guide to keep them effective. **If you've found this book useful, please consider leaving a short review on Amazon. it would mean a lot.Copyright**

If you've found this book useful, please select five stars on Amazon. Knowing I helped you save money in New York would mean genuinely make my day.

Copyright

Printed in Great Britain
by Amazon

19129367R00119